THE ONION PICKER

Sugar Ray Robinson *(left)* and Carmen Basilio going toe to
toe at Yankee Stadium, September 23, 1957.
Courtesy of Carmen Basilio.

The ONION PICKER

CARMEN BASILIO
& Boxing in the 1950s

GARY B. YOUMANS

Campbell Road Press, North

The paper used in this publication meets the minimum requirements
of American National Standard for Information Sciences—
Permanence of Paper for Printed Library Materials, ANSI Z39.48–1984.∞™

ISBN-13: 978-0-8156-8175-5   ISBN-10: 0-8156-8175-5

Produced and distributed by Syracuse University Press
Syracuse, New York 13244-5160.

For a listing of books published and distributed by Syracuse University
Press, visit our Web site at SyracuseUniversityPress.syr.edu.

Manufactured in the United States of America

To Nat Rosasco and Carmen Scialabba,
two very special people in the lives
of Carmen and Josie Basilio

Gary B. Youmans grew up in Syracuse, New York, where he developed his long-standing love of sports. After playing basketball at Ashland College in Ohio, he went on to coach high school basketball in Florida and professional basketball in the Continental Basketball Association and in Canada. He has even owned a minor league basketball team. Gary has co-authored two previous books, *'59: The Story of the 1959 Syracuse University National Championship Football Team* and *'63: The Story of the 1963 World Champion Chicago Bears.*

Contents

Illustrations

Preface

the old man moves a little slower now as he passes his eightieth round on earth. The memory isn't always there, but ask him a question about boxing, and it delivers like an overhand left to Tony DeMarco's jaw. He handled heart disease back in 1992 just like he handled being robbed of the welterweight title in 1956: he dealt with it and moved on.

Carmen Basilio remains alive and well though many of his compatriots have passed on. That mug of his easily gives him away to the legion of fans who remember when he battled the best of the best. His voice, a cross somewhere between Vito Corleone and Jimmy Durante, gravels at you in a staccato style: "What's your name, kid? Where you from? Don't mess with me—I'm still a tough guy." Then comes the sly grin followed by an extended right hand. His handshake is firm, quick to the point, something that has been practiced thousands of times since he retired from the ring in 1961. He bonds easily with the people who come up to say hello and get his autograph. If you engage him in talk about boxing you can expect three quick right jabs followed by a left cross stopping a few inches from your nose. This old pug is comfortable in his own skin and genuinely likes people—well, let's say he likes *most* people.

It has been fifty years since he beat Ray Robinson in Yankee Stadium for the middleweight championship, but mention Sugar Ray to him and his jaw tightens. "Don't talk about that bastard to me. I got no use for him" is an automatic response. "I didn't like him then, and I don't like him now. That's the way I feel about him. Call me a jerk, fine, but that's the way I feel about him."

Time is supposed to mellow great athletes as they reflect on their special moments in time. Genuine disdain that they may have had for their opponents is typically washed away as they grow older. Paying respect to their partners in history is the politically correct thing to do—giving a man his due. Being conciliatory toward your fellow competitors is something we have come to expect from our heroes. Ali-Frazier, Zale-Graziano, Pep-Saddler all became more civil to each other with time. But Carmen Basilio feels no need to throw an olive branch to his most bitter opponent, Sugar Ray Robinson. That is not who he is. That is not how he has lived his life. He is an honest, straightforward, simple man. What you see is what you get.

There was that time down in Florida when he was told he was welcome but his black sparring partners were not. He told them, "If they don't stay here, neither do I." Accommodations were made for the entire Basilio party. He has earned his place in boxing history for what he accomplished in the ring and the way he conducted himself outside that ring. He believed when the battle was over, you were gracious to your opponent and the people around him. But that sentiment ends when it comes to Sugar Ray Robinson. He thinks Robinson was arrogant, so self-absorbed that he cared little about other people. Basilio has never questioned Robinson's talent. Hell, he was in the ring with him.

There was a time in New York in the early 1950s when he approached Robinson and was snubbed. Robinson walked past him without so much as a hello.

ANNA BASILIO BAXTER (Sister): "We were in New York to attend a Sugar Ray Robinson fight. We were walking into the hotel when Carmen spotted a car pulling up. He said, 'Wait, here comes Sugar Ray. I want to meet him.' Well, Carmen walks up, and Sugar Ray just pushes him aside like he was not there. He never acknowledged Carmen at all. It was demeaning to Carmen, and, boy, was he mad. He said, 'One day I'll get even with that guy.'"

CARMEN BASILIO: "He just acted like I wasn't there. He dissed me. I had never treated other people like that in my entire life. He could have said hello, or something. I said to myself that one day I'm going to kick that guy's ass. Then he will know who the hell I am."

JOHN DEJOHN (Trainer): "Carmen has great affection for people, but they have to meet his standards. He is one of the most discerning guys in the world. He likes real people and can pick out a phony a mile away."

The great Sugar Ray Robinson was in his second decade of a magnificent career when he agreed to fight Carmen Basilio in September 1957. He needed money, and fighting the current welterweight champion would secure a good payday. Although his superior boxing skills were eroding, Robinson still had enough in his arsenal to beat the best boxers of the mid-1950s. Styles make fights, and Robinson believed he could beat Basilio, though he knew it would come at a price. Basilio could go to the body like nobody else he had fought in the past few years. This guy was a warrior. In his mind he could win this war, but it would be a tough, physical fight, a toe-to-toe donnybrook.

Earlier in 1957, Robinson had avenged his loss to Gene Fullmer by knocking him out with one punch in the first round. "The punch" quieted most of his critics who questioned whether he still had his punching power. He hoped he could catch Basilio early with one of those lethal blows. Otherwise, he was going to have to work much harder and absorb a lot of punishment to put away another contender in a long list of contenders. The sport bored him, but it was the one sure way to earn any real money. And he needed money. He always needed money. He was Sugar Ray Robinson, the greatest boxer in the history of the sport. Whacking this onion picker from Canastota, New York, was necessary. He had to have the dough. The IRS was hounding him. Batter up.

Acknowledgments

everyone I spoke with regarding this book gave of their time to share how special a person Carmen Basilio is and how he has touched their lives.

Thanks to my wife, Caroline, who did much of the word processing for the manuscript and special thanks to Annette "the Hammer" Wenda for excellent copyediting and keeping me on track. Thanks to Ed Brophy at the Boxing Hall of Fame for his introductions to Carmen and his wife, Josie. Also, as always, a big thank-you to the folks at Syracuse University Press who provide so much help in the creation of a book.

Thanks also goes out to Ross Stagnitti for his extra efforts in organizing some interviews with Carmen Basilio's family and friends.

I would also like to thank others who contributed to this book, including Donnie Hamilton, Greg Sorrentino, Ada Rothschild, Angelo Dundee, Anna Basilio Baxter, and countless others who helped me in my research for *The Onion Picker*.

Finally, a special thanks to Carmen and his lovely wife, Josie, who graciously accepted me into their home and provided me with wonderful stories and pictures of Carmen's career.

I take full responsibility for all errors of omission and commission, misstatements, and other inaccuracies in telling this story. If it's wrong, it's my error.

THE ONION PICKER

1. Carmen Basilio on the family farm, circa 1960.
Courtesy of Carmen Basilio.

1.

The Onion Picker

The promise of America is a simple promise: Every person shall share in the blessings of this land.

—LYNDON B. JOHNSON

in early April 1904, seventeen years old, Giuseppe Basile boarded the ship *Germania* to set sail across the Atlantic Ocean for the United States. Traveling alone, he was headed to a place called West Virginia, where a new life working in the coal mines awaited him. Giuseppe, like so many other Italian immigrants in the early 1900s, was in pursuit of the American dream. He hoped the pilgrimage to this new land would present a bridge to a better life.

Italy had become one of the most overcrowded countries in Europe at the turn of the century. Many Italians, because of low wages and high taxes, were fleeing the country in record numbers and heading to the United States. From 1890 to 1900, 655,000 Italian immigrants arrived in America, two-thirds of them men. For many of these Italian immigrants, the migration to the United States was not so much a rejection of their homeland as a temporary move to hold on to their Italian way of life. Many of these immigrants hoped to save enough money in America to eventually return to a better life in Italy. Young Giuseppe Basile joined these "birds of passage" as they headed to what they believed was the land of plenty.

Arriving at Ellis Island on April 28, 1904, Manifest Line no. 0020 was nervous, but mostly apprehensive as he waited in a long line with thousands of other immigrants hoping for admission to America. He watched in horror as a number of people were turned away at the gate. Giuseppe prayed that this would not become his fate, as his family had gambled everything to finance his journey to the United States. There were no options for him to return home. He had to make the best of it regardless of how hard life may become. He would learn to cope in this land, carving out an existence however possible. Someday he would return to his native land.

Giuseppe passed the time in line talking with a friend he had met on the boat, Alphonso Fuschillo. Alphonso, who was a year older than Giuseppe, was also headed for West Virginia and a job as a coal miner. The two young immigrants quickly became fast friends, sharing their hopes and dreams of what lay ahead. There were so many unknown and unanswered questions about their future. Everything would work out. It had to. It just had to.

"Next. Come, young man. Let's go. I don't have all day." Giuseppe quickly gathered his belongings and proceeded toward the impatient man in the dark uniform. The stern inspector looked Giuseppe up and down and motioned for him to turn around. Jotting down notes on a wooden clipboard, he asked Giuseppe to place his cardboard suitcase on a table in front of him. Shuffling through Giuseppe's belongings, he asked the startled youngster three questions: "Where are you going? Who paid for your passage? Do you have a job waiting for you?" Giuseppe tried not to appear nervous and answered each of the three questions with as much confidence as he could muster. While writing down each of Giuseppe's responses on his clipboard, the inspector told Giuseppe not to move, that he would be right back.

After what seemed like an eternity, the inspector returned with another man who asked Giuseppe if he had ever been arrested. Feeling his body begin to tremble, barely able to speak, he finally blurted out, "No . . . never . . . No, Mr. Inspector, I have never been in trouble. I have a letter—." The second man stopped him in midsentence. "That's all right. We have all we need. He's okay. Pass him through."

Giuseppe was directed to a line in the corner of the huge building and was instructed to wait there. When he reached the end of the long line, the young boy took off his cap and knelt down to thank God for watching over him. Relieved to have passed through immigration, he now watched as his friend Alphonso was interrogated by the same inspector. Alphonso passed through much quicker than Giuseppe had, and the two boys embraced, both elated to have been accepted into America. They were now on their way to West Virginia and the business of coal mining.

When the train carrying Giuseppe and Alphonso arrived in West Virginia, the two young men found a world much different from what they had expected. The living conditions they were forced to live in bordered on uninhabitable. The coal company provided their housing, which consisted of rough lumber with no indoor plumbing. They were paid by company money called "scrip" that was exchangeable only at the company store. Giuseppe was required to furnish his own tools, which he did not have. He would be able to purchase them on credit from the company store, which quickly put him in debt. If he needed medical treatment, a medical doctor was provided, and the doctor's services were deducted from his wages. Many weeks, the amount of his paycheck was little or nothing. Giuseppe persevered and learned to make his dollars stretch by sharing living expenses with Alphonso. On Sunday after mass, they would wash their clothes, then enjoy their one day off with the other Italian families. Some weeks, they would be required to work on Sunday, which they did without complaint.

The work in the mines has been described as the meanest in the world. Twelve hours a day, six days a week, the workers toiled under the ground, dealing with smoke, bad air, and cold, damp conditions. Giuseppe would work the entire duration of his shift stooped over, laboring on his knees in a puddle of water. Taking in the coal dust all day affected his breathing, but he never complained. Over a period of time the coal dust could destroy the air sacs of a miner's lungs. This condition, a shortness of breath, later became known as black lung disease. For years the coal companies refused to recognize black lung as a valid medical problem caused by poor working conditions. They had company doctors diagnose respiratory disorders as anything but black lung. One doctor told an unsuspecting Giuseppe that breathing coal dust was actually good for him. Giuseppe was paid forty cents a ton, with a projected annual income of a little more than six hundred dollars.

After being in West Virginia for a short time, Giuseppe decided that he would change his name to make it sound more American. Many of the Italian miners had convinced him that changing his name would make everything easier. Many of the miners had Americanized versions of their names. After pondering for a few days what his new name should be, he decided on Basilio. Joseph Basilio would be his new American name, and for days he walked around the mines introducing himself to everyone he came in contact with. "My name is Joseph Basilio. I am very happy to meet you." The pride he felt in the Basilio name never changed his entire life.

Joseph never complained about the grueling work but dreamed of one day working aboveground rather than spending his life in a deep, dark cave. His dreams were answered when his friend Alphonso Fuschillo told him of farming work that was available in New York State. He told Joseph that he had received a letter from his cousin who was working there. His cousin said that the farmers were hiring everyone who showed up. Alphonso wasn't sure exactly what they would be farming, but it had to be better work than coal mining. Joseph jumped at the chance to leave the mines and work in fresh air and sunlight. He packed the few belongings he had and headed for this new place called Canastota.

The village of Canastota is located in Madison County, twenty-five miles east of Syracuse, New York. In the early twentieth century the population soared, as vegetable farms sprang up in and around this small hamlet situated near the Erie Canal. The climate and the area's rich black soil provided perfect growing conditions for vegetable farming. The soil contained high concentrations of decomposed organic matter and minerals, making it extremely fertile.

Onions became the crown jewel, and young Joseph Basilio quickly learned how to farm the mucky soil.

Joseph lived with an Italian family when he first arrived in Canastota. The Capparellis lived in town and introduced him to Mary Picciano, whose father, Cosmo, had emigrated to the United States in 1896 from Italy. The young couple began dating and fell in love. Joseph and Mary were married in St. Agatha's Church on November 25, 1909. Joseph had saved enough money to buy Mary a twenty-four-carat gold ring, which he purchased for six dollars at the jewelry store located on Peterboro Street in downtown Canastota.

Mary and Joseph were excited about their future in America. Creating a strong family life with many children was important to both of them. The young newlyweds took up residence in a small shack on a farm during the growing season. Sharecropping fifteen acres, they worked seven days a week, from sunup to sundown. From late March through late September they were up at five o'clock in the morning tending their crops. The hot summer sun heated the soil and burned their hands and feet, but they never complained.

In September, when the final onion was harvested, they shared their bounty equally with the landowner. One onion for them, and one onion for the landowner. Some years were better than others. The central New York weather could play havoc with their crops. Too much rain, a hailstorm, a strong wind . . . any of these could spell disaster for the crops. Joseph and Mary persevered with their strong faith in God and genuine love for each other. It got them through the tough times.

The couple's first two attempts to have children failed, and both were lost during Mary's pregnancy. Finally, daughter Jessie was born, with a second daughter, Lucy, born a year later. Life in central New York State was improving, but Joseph still yearned to see his mother and father in Italy. In 1917, following the growing season, the Basilio family visited Italy for what they thought would be a short stay.

2. Joseph Basilio in Italian military uniform.
Courtesy of Carmen Basilio.

ANNA BASILIO BAXTER (Sister): "My parents traveled back to Italy, where they got caught in the First World War. My father was drafted into the Italian army and served on the side of the Allies. My mother was pregnant with my sister Matilda when they arrived in Italy. Later, I was conceived there, making me the only Basilio child conceived and born in Italy. We were there five years."

When Joseph was mustered out of the Italian Army in 1922, the family made immediate plans to return to Canastota. Joseph wanted to resume onion farming, only this time he was going to work for himself. He had saved enough to put down money on ten acres a few miles outside of town. There was a monthly mortgage that needed to be paid, but at least he would no longer be working for someone else. The work was hard, but the family survived and continued to grow, as daughter number five, Nellie, was born, prior to Mary presenting Joseph with his first son, Armondo. Two years later the Basilio family had their second son, as Carman Cosmo Basilio entered the world on April 2, 1927. Paul, Delores, and Joey would follow over the next few years, making a total of ten children in the Basilio family, six girls and four boys.

ANNA BASILIO BAXTER (Sister): "My father was the best man you could ever meet. He was a great person. He loved his family. My mother was small, like we were, but when she spoke, it was the law. There was always food on the table. At night when all the work was done, my mother would sit down and read the paper cover to cover. She could read and write, besides being able to speak Italian and English. My father could not read or write, so she would read Pa the news each night. He would sit in his chair, quietly listening to her read the paper to him. They spoke Italian between the two of them, but only English to us kids. None of us ever learned how to speak Italian. I guess Ma and Pa wanted us to be more Americanized."

CARMEN BASILIO: "My father was a good man. Tough. Very strict. He didn't talk a lot, but when he did, you had better listen. He liked to have a glass of his homemade wine at night. Each year he would make four or five barrels of the stuff. He would send me down to the cellar to get his wine. I loved going down to the cellar to get his wine because then I could take a shot myself."

One winter Joseph found work on the New York Railroad, which helped provide income for the family. Despite his heavy workload, Joseph found time to hunt and fish the woodlands and streams around Canastota. He also became interested in sports, particularly boxing. Each Friday night he would listen to the broadcast of the fights on the radio, and the Basilio family would gather around to listen to the exploits of Jack Dempsey, Joe Louis, and Joseph's favorite fighter, Jim Braddock.

ANNA BASILIO BAXTER (Sister): "On Fridays we could stay up a little later to listen to the fights with my father. We got so we

3. A young Carmen Basilio, circa 1935.
Courtesy of Carmen Basilio.

knew all the fighters and enjoyed listening to the broadcast. We couldn't so much as breathe. We had to be very quiet so Pa could hear what was going on."

When Carmen was four years old, he was taught by his older sisters how to write his name. They spelled his name C-A-R-M-E-N, the feminine way, instead of C-A-R-M-A-N, the masculine way.

CARMEN BASILIO: "The spelling of my first name has a lot to do with my sisters. They taught me to spell it with an *e* all of the time. On my birth certificate it is C-A-R-M-A-N. When I went to get my driver's license when I was sixteen years old, I wrote down C-A-R-M-E-N. I never changed it."

4. Young Basilio brothers boxing.
Courtesy of Carmen Basilio.

When Carmen was six years old, Joseph bought his sons two pairs of boxing gloves. He fixed up a corner of the cellar as a ring where the brothers could go at it. His love of boxing quickly spilled over to his sons, and they could be found each day boxing in the cellar. The boys, time and again, would come upstairs all bloodied, and Mother Basilio would have a fit. She would yell at her husband for being the root cause of this family warfare. He would smile and say, "It's okay, Ma. One day they will be champions."

During the summertime with the family living at the farm, the Basilio children walked three miles each day to school. Their spring break each year was dependent on the weather. If it was warm enough to begin planting, school was out of session. If the weather remained cold, the school holiday would have to wait until it warmed up. Each day the children would work in the onion fields.

CARMEN BASILIO: "The last word we would hear in the morning when you left to go to school was, 'Get home quick. We got a lot of work to do.'"

ANNA BASILIO BAXTER (Sister): "Sometimes when we were walking home from school, we would hear a car coming, and we would hide so they wouldn't pick us up. We knew when we got home, we would go right to work. All us kids worked on the farm. My father on Saturdays would cut wood, and we kids would stack it. Also on Saturdays we would clean the ashes out of the furnace in the cellar. We had to have all our chores done by one o'clock, because that is when we all had to go to confession so we would be able to take communion on Sunday. We all had certain jobs that we had to do. My oldest sister, Jessie, did most of the heavy cleaning. My sister Lucy was in charge of the ironing. Matilda, Tillie, and I would help Ma with the dishes, peeling potatoes, or whatever needed to be done to prepare our meals. The boys were young at that time, so they were excused from daily chores, but that changed as they got older."

Each spring the Basilio children were down on their hands and knees in the muck, planting onion stubs the size of their little fingers. Without realizing it, during his whole adolescence Carmen was strengthening his legs, hips, and stomach muscles, which would pay huge dividends down the road.

CARMEN BASILIO: "We hated it . . . but who likes to work when you're a kid?"

While Carmen was in elementary school, a teacher who had boxed at Syracuse University decided to share his passion for the sport with his young students. He formed a team that fought a series of preliminary fights prior to the high school boxing team's matches. It was the future middleweight champion of the world's first taste of participation in an organized match.

CARMEN BASILIO: "When I was asked by my fourth grade teacher what I wanted to be in life, I told her that I wanted to be a boxing champion. The class all laughed. She thought that was the most disgusting thing she had ever heard, but I didn't care, because that's what I wanted to do. I remember in elementary school I fought a kid named Goodsell. Funny, I have never forgot that. I won by TKO [technical knockout] in the second round. My older brother, Armondo, was on the high school boxing team at the time, and I couldn't wait to get to high school so I could get on the team."

When Carmen did reach high school, he quickly became the best eighty-five-pound boxer on the best boxing team Canastota High School ever had. The country was now becoming deeply involved in World War II, with rationing felt everywhere. All school athletic programs at Canastota High School were suspended indefinitely. When there was no more boxing team, Carmen Basilio on his sixteenth birthday decided to quit school. A year later Carmen went to his parents to ask permission to enlist in the U.S. Marines Corps. His brother Armondo was already a marine, and Carmen pleaded with his parents to allow him to join his brother. His mother was totally against her second son also becoming a soldier.

CARMEN BASILIO: "They were not too happy about me joining the marines. I had to talk them into it. I told them they had better sign me up, because in another year when I became eighteen they would draft me. At least this way I have some choice in the branch of service I went into. If I waited, I had no choice. They signed, and I was off to the war."

First stop Parris Island, South Carolina, where Carmen Basilio was indoctrinated into the ways of the Marine Corps. Reveille at 0500, breakfast, PT, classes, drill twice a day, weapons cleaning, Carmen thrived in the discipline of boot camp. He approached becoming a marine with the same resolve and attitude that carried him through his entire career as a professional fighter.

CARMEN BASILIO: "I was ready for boot camp, although the training was hard. I was in better shape than most of the guys because of my boxing [training]. I got a chance to box when I was in boot camp. They had me box this kid, and I handled him pretty good. Then they had me box someone else, and I handled him pretty good. Then all of a sudden I got to be a boxing star with the platoon because I handled everybody I boxed."

When boot camp was completed, the next stop for Basilio's platoon was Camp Lejeune, North Carolina, for combat training.

After seven months of intense training, it was on to Camp Pendleton in California, where they would wait for orders to be shipped overseas. Three days before Carmen's platoon was to ship out, the atomic bomb was dropped, ending the war. Basilio's platoon was reassigned to Guam to guard Japanese prisoners of war.

CARMEN BASILIO: "When I got to Camp Pendleton they had a boxing team, so I got involved with that. There was this guy named Jerry Plunkett who was a good boxer that trained me. He had been a champion boxer in the service. His idea of training us was to beat the shit out of us in the ring. He helped me get on some cards while I was there. He ended up being a twenty-five-year man with the marines. We stayed in touch after the war."

JERRY PLUNKETT: "Carmen was a little awkward when he first started sparring with me, but he had tremendous determination, and I encouraged him. After a while he began to belt me pretty good. I knew then that he would make a name for himself in boxing after the war."

CARMEN BASILIO: "The Japanese prisoners were no trouble. I was good to them myself. At that time you had to wash your own clothes. I would say to them, 'You want a job? You want to earn a pack of cigarettes? You wash my clothes, and I will give you a pack of cigarettes.' A pack of cigarettes was six cents at the time."

In late 1947, Carmen Basilio received an honorable discharge from the marines and headed home to Canastota. He went to work in nearby Rome, New York, for the General Cable Company as a machinist. Each day when Carmen finished work he went to the local gym, where he would work out hitting the punching bags, shadowboxing, and occasionally sparring a couple of rounds. He would end his three hours of training with a four-mile run. Every day he worked out, never considering taking a day off or easing up on his training schedule.

CARMEN BASILIO: "Each morning I would go to communion before I went to work in Rome for the General Cable Company. After work I would go and work out at the gym. My mother would say, 'Forget that dirty, rotten game.' I would tell her, 'Ma, that's what I want to be, that's want I want to do . . . I am going to be a world champion.' Nobody was going to change my mind about that."

Carmen was determined to become a professional boxer and maintained his routine for six months before moving his training to Syracuse. He felt isolated in Rome, away from the fight game. Moving his training to Syracuse, he believed, would give him a better chance of getting noticed. It was there that he met Sammy Ashmer, a former boxer out of Utica who began to work with him. He helped arrange Carmen's first fight as a professional in Binghamton, New York, on November 24, 1948. Carmen drew a veteran boxer named Jimmy Evans in his professional debut. Pressuring Evans from the opening bell, Basilio caught him with a left hook in the third round, knocking him down. Evans survived the count, but the referee stopped the bout a short time later, as Basilio mauled the defenseless Evans in the corner.

CARMEN BASILIO: "I felt great that I had won. I'd seen him fight before as a pro. He'd been around a long time, he was an old-timer, but he wasn't aggressive enough. I was nervous. That never changed. If you're not nervous, you're in trouble. If you're nervous, then you're sharp and you're alert."

In his second professional fight, Carmen Basilio knocked out his opponent, Bruce Walters, in the first round. Carmen would fight twice more in 1948, winning once by knockout over his opponent Eddie Thomas, then winning a hard-fought six-round decision over Rollie Johns in Syracuse.

CARMEN BASILIO: "When I started out I made fifty to seventy-five dollars a fight. If I had a couple of guys in the corner, I would give them thirty bucks, and they would split it. I was having fun doing what I wanted to do. I was still working at the cable company during the day and chasing my dream at night."

Basilio would stay active in 1949, fighting and winning three times in January and once in February to run his record to 8-0. On May 2, 1949, he suffered his first loss, losing a close six-round decision to the more experienced Connie Thies in Rochester, New

York. Basilio fought nine more times in 1949, winning eight, five by knockout. He was winning and still chasing his dream as the decade of the 1950s approached.

ANNA BASILIO BAXTER (Sister): "Every year my father would have a garden and grow beefsteak tomatoes. This one year he had two tomatoes that grew into the shape of boxing gloves. I remember he said it was a sign that Carmen was going to be a champion."

5. A young Basilio training at Irv Robbins's gym.
Courtesy of Don Hamilton.

2.

The Early Years

in the early 1950s Americans were purchasing goods and services at a record pace. Sixty-four percent of the population still lived in cities, but that number was changing as suburban housing was sprouting up across the country. Gasoline was twenty-seven cents a gallon, bread fourteen cents a loaf, and you could still mail a letter for three cents. The minimum wage was up to seventy-five cents an hour, as new jobs were created to meet the demand for more products. Growth was being seen everywhere.

Radio was still the main source for music, news, and sports in 1950, but national sponsors were beginning to leave radio for television at record rates. In January 1950 there was a little more than five million television sets in the United States. That number would double by the end of the year and rapidly expand each succeeding year for the remainder of the decade. Arthur Godfrey and Faye Emerson were voted the top personalities on television in 1950, with Milton Berle's *Texaco Star Theater* rated the number-one show.

The sport of boxing was enjoying a growth period during 1950 as more and more fighters returned from the war to resume their boxing careers. Small fight clubs sprang up across the country, providing venues for fighters to hone their craft. Young boxers such as Tony DeMarco, Johnny Saxton, Joey Giardello, and Carmen Basilio could fight every few days, many times squaring off against the same opponent. Tony DeMarco fought eight times in 1950, Saxton ten times; Basilio had eleven fights, and Giardello, one of

6. Sugar Ray Robinson.
Courtesy of AP Images.

the busiest of boxers, fought sixteen times in 1950. It seemed that every small town in the United States had a weekly fight card with an ample supply of combatants.

Sugar Ray Robinson was also a busy boxer in 1950, fighting nineteen times, defeating all his opponents, twelve by way of knockout. He began the year scoring a TKO over George LaRover in four rounds in New Haven, Connecticut, then finished the year on Christmas Day in Frankfurt, Germany, knocking out Hans Stretz. In between he defended his world welterweight crown three times, besides winning the Pennsylvania middleweight title by knocking out Bobo Olsen in Philadelphia. *Ring Magazine*'s founder, Nat Fleischer, placed Robinson at the head of the class in 1950, saying at the time, "He is the greatest all around fighter, pound for pound in any division."

Ray Robinson as an amateur fighter showed glimpses that he was no ordinary boxer. Undefeated in eighty-five fights, sixty-nine by knockout, he began to garner much attention in the late 1930s. He dominated the Golden Gloves, winning both the featherweight and the lightweight titles, with the majority of his fights not lasting past the first round. His style so smooth, there was a rhythm to his boxing, demonstrating his amazing balance of coordination, timing, and power. He was an artist . . . a Caruso in boxing gloves. He took this roughest of sports to a level that had never been seen before. *Perfection* is a term that probably described Robinson's boxing style during this time period. His combinations were flawless, delivered with speed and accuracy, a variety of punches that rained down hell on his opponents. Robinson had not lost a match since 1943, when Jake La Motta beat him in Detroit. Robinson turned the tables on La Motta three weeks later in a lightning-quick rematch, beating the Raging Bull over ten rounds, again in the Motor City.

Jake La Motta and Ray Robinson, for the sixth and final time, would face off in Chicago on February 14, 1951. Sugar Ray had won four times, La Motta once in their previous battles. This final installment would again play out in Chicago, with the International Boxing Club (IBC) selecting a most fitting date for this final battle . . . St. Valentine's Day.

Jake La Motta was the current, reigning middleweight champion in 1951, having taken the title from Marcel Cerdan in June 1949. The French champion had dislocated his arm in the first round against La Motta, but gamely fought on through nine rounds before his corner convinced him to stop. Fighting with one hand, Cerdan battled La Motta with courage and conviction before not coming out for the tenth round. Sadly, it would be the popular Frenchman's last fight, as he would die a few months later in an airplane crash. While returning to the United States in an attempt to regain the title from La Motta, Cerdan's Air France plane crashed in the Azores, killing everyone on board. He was thirty-three years old.

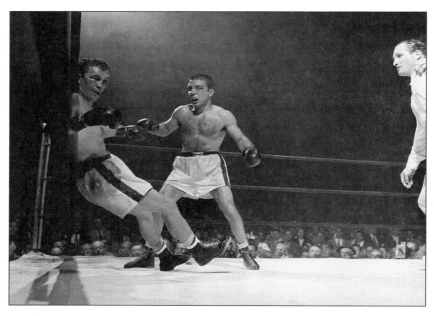

7. Jake La Motta delivering a knockout blow to challenger Laurent Dauthuille in the fifteenth round. *Courtesy of AP Images.*

Jake La Motta, similar to other fighters of his era, turned to boxing as a way out of a tough life. His father introduced him to the sport by having him fight other kids in his neighborhood. He would tell his son, "Jake, hit 'em first . . . and hit 'em hard." La Motta was in and out of trouble throughout the early part of his life, and boxing became his path to fame and fortune.

JAKE LA MOTTA (Boxer): "The first thing you got to do if you want to be a fighter is fight. I figured that out by the time I got to the amateurs. I'd already had a thousand fights. If you're fighting all the time, besides learning how to do it, you get so a fight doesn't make any difference one way or the other. The fact of the matter is you get to liking fighting. At least I did."

Jake La Motta turned professional in 1941, fighting an amazing twenty times during his first year in boxing, winning eighteen, three by knockout. By 1942 *Ring Magazine* ranked him as the sixth-best middleweight in the world. Throughout the early 1940s he continued to box well, taking on all comers, which included future Hall of Fame boxers Sugar Ray Robinson and Fritzie Zivic. He fought Zivic four times over a seven-month period between 1943 and 1944, winning three of those contests. Despite having success against top fighters, La Motta still couldn't get a shot at the middleweight belt. Finally in 1947, with his career stalled, he made a deal with the devil to get his title match. La Motta agreed to take a dive in a fight against Billy Fox. The Mob was grooming Fox for a run at the light heavyweight title and believed a victory over La Motta, the toughest of fighters, would enhance his reputation with the public. The fight took place at Madison Square Garden on November 14, 1947. La Motta offered little resistance from the opening bell, settling on the ropes, where Fox pounded him at will. By the fourth round the referee had seen enough of this one-sided match and stopped it. The fight was scored a TKO for Fox, although La Motta never hit the canvas.

RED SMITH (Writer): "La Motta, the Bronx Bull, was as tough as any man of his time. He had agreed to a barney to ornament the gaudy record of one Blackjack Billy Fox. Jake had never been off his feet before and was too proud to hit the deck. He floundered along the ropes impersonating a carp out of water until a faint-hearted referee stopped the performance."

Whispers of a fix quickly spread through the Garden, as La Motta gave a putrid performance for a legitimate fighter that night. He had built a reputation on his ring toughness. Void of great boxing skills, La Motta would battle you anyway he could to win. Jake was a brawler. Few people in the Garden who watched that night bought into his performance against Fox.

JAKE LA MOTTA (Boxer): "I purposely lost to Billy Fox because they promised me I would get a shot at the title if I did. Today it is a little different. If a fellow deserves a chance at the title, the people will argue for it. In my time there were lots of guys that deserved chances to fight for the title. There were a lot of uncrowned champs around at that time that didn't get the shot. Those were the guys I had to fight because nobody else wanted to fight them."

In La Motta's mind it was a clear and simple business decision. If mobsters Frankie Carbo and Blinky Palermo were going to control boxing without being challenged by the legitimate boxing community, then he would do what was ultimately best for him. It would cost him a win against a bum he thought he could beat, but so what, in the grand scheme of things? He wanted his shot at the belt, something he believed he had earned and deserved. His goal since he had started fighting for dough was to become a champion. Jake convinced himself that any road would do in achieving that goal. Two years later Jake La Motta fought the ill-fated Cerdan, and his dream came true.

JAKE LA MOTTA (Boxer): "I cannot describe exactly what I felt. I felt like God had given me the world. It was absolute pandemonium. There was booing—I could hear that—but the whole place was filled with cheering, cheering for me, the reform-school kid from the Bronx."

La Motta waited more than a year before defending his middleweight title, choosing to fight four nontitle bouts, winning three and losing one. He decisioned Tiberio Mitri in the first defense of his crown in New York on July 12, 1950. Despite defeating Mitri, who at the time was the European middleweight champion, he was getting heat from the boxing world to fight a top contender.

Sugar Ray Robinson, the reigning welterweight champion, was the people's choice. La Motta agreed to fight Robinson, but it would have to be in 1951 for tax purposes. First, he would take on Laurent Dauthuille in Detroit, a fighter he had lost a close ten-round decision to in 1949. Once finished with Dauthuille, he would turn his attention to fighting Robinson in early 1951. Jake was getting as much mileage as he could out of being a middleweight champion, picking up some easy cash before having a big payday against his toughest opponent, Sugar Ray Robinson.

Jake La Motta, clearly unprepared to defend his title that night in Detroit, almost lost to Laurent Dauthuille, who fought the fight of his career. Trailing badly as the fight entered the fifteenth round, Jake pulled off one of the great comebacks in boxing history. Pretending to be in trouble, La Motta tricked the Frenchman into coming in close to finish him off. La Motta attacked the surprised Dauthuille with everything he had, finishing him off with a series of well-timed blows to the body and head.

JAKE LA MOTTA (Boxer): "I came out for the fifteenth knowing what I had to do, charging at him, throwing left and rights. He knew he had the fight won, and he tried to cover up against me, and I tried to keep boring in, getting more and more desperate as the round went on. Suddenly, in the midst of one mixup I threw a left hook, one of the few I had thrown all night, and by pure luck he was wide open at that moment. The punch caught him flush on the jaw. I saw him sag and start to back away, and I followed him, throwing punches as hard and as fast as I could. I saw that he was gone."

ARTHUR DALEY (Writer): "Jake put his title on the line against another Frenchman, Laurent Dauthuille, only this Frenchman can't fight. He's a busy little guy who swings often and furiously, but even his most violent punch couldn't dent a cream puff. Despite that handicap he had the Bronx Bull over a barrel, as soundly beaten a fighter as ever entered a ring, as he whisked into the final round. Since folks trust Jake as much as they can throw a Hereford Bull, it began to look like a barney, except no one could understand why Jake would throw away a championship of which he is so proud. Thereupon the unpredictable La Motta saved everything, including his honor, by knocking out Dauthuille a scant thirteen seconds before the final bell."

●　　●　　●

CHICAGO, FEBRUARY 14, 1951. A crowd of 14,802 watched Sugar Ray Robinson end Jake La Motta's time as middleweight champion, as he battered his longtime foe into a bloody pulp. The end came in the thirteenth when referee Frank Sikora stopped the massacre with fifty-six seconds to go in the round. La Motta, defenseless against the ropes, was being pounded at will by Robinson. The Bronx Bull left the ring battered and bruised but never toppled to the canvas. His record of never being knocked off his feet or KO'd remained intact. Under Illinois boxing rules, the win by Robinson went into the record books as a "technical knockout" instead of a knockout. La Motta was as beaten as any fighter, laying on the canvas, out cold. Later he collapsed in his dressing room and was on oxygen for more than an hour.

JAKE LA MOTTA (Boxer): "Robinson had me but I wouldn't give the son of a bitch the satisfaction of knocking me down. I told the referee I'd murder him if he tried to stop the fight. I got my arm wedged around one of the ring ropes and stayed there, defying Robinson to knock me down. He couldn't, but I got about as bad a beating as I ever had."

Sugar Ray Robinson, now the middleweight champion, was forced to relinquish his welterweight crown. Dual ownerships of boxing titles were no longer possible because it was believed it caused too much confusion with the public. Since 1938, when Henry Armstrong owned three titles, it had been decided that when a fighter went up in class and won a title, he would automatically be forced to relinquish the lighter crown.

GEORGE GAINFORD (Robinson Trainer): "I resent commissions taking away titles they give no one. They didn't give Ray the welterweight title . . . he won it in the ring. That's the only place he can lose it."

The new middleweight champion looked forward to some rest after having fought eighteen times over the previous twelve months. He received $20,555 for his efforts and $1,500 from the televised fight. The deposed champion took home $61,111 and the $1,500 from television. Jake La Motta the next day showed the visual effects of the beating he had taken from Robinson, saying he was more tired and sore than anything else. La Motta thought his problems getting down to the 160-pound weight limit had affected his performance. He was coy about another championship match with Sugar Ray, saying he would like to fight him at 170 pounds.

Robinson toyed with the idea of moving up another class and challenging light heavyweight champion Joey Maxim for his crown, possibly late in 1951, in New York. Those plans would be put on hold, as another trip overseas and an unfortunate meeting with an Englishman named Randy Turpin took precedence.

* * *

Carmen Basilio entered the 1950s with his dream of becoming a champion intact and pushing him forward. He was never interested in making a hundred bucks beating a man's scull in or, worse yet, getting his own scull kicked in. He was there to win, to move to the main event. Someday become somebody, someday become a champion, that's where the money was, and that's where his dreams lay. Working a job by day and fighting at night was a temporary situation, but accepting the poverty of a preliminary fighter was never for him—he believed he was better than that. If it turned out he wasn't, he would leave, but that wasn't going to happen, because he wouldn't let it happen. He would get his work done in the gym, he would find the right trainer, someone who could help him. He would outwork, outfight, any man alive. Those smelly changing rooms that a preliminary fighter shared with ten other fighters were nothing more than a night at a cheap hotel.

Preliminary fighters changed jobs to keep their dreams alive. Washing dishes one week, driving a delivery truck the next, always changing jobs so they can take the next fight, keeping the dream alive, many times never quitting until it was too late. Money most days was scarce. Sometimes they had to ask for favors. Those who stayed too long got their faces pushed in, their brains scrambled. Scar tissue formed around the eyes where hair used to grow. The wins meant nothing, and nobody cared if they lost. That's what Carmen Basilio was in 1950: a preliminary fighter trying to move up or move out.

DONNIE HAMILTON (Boxing Historian): "I was ten years old when I first met Carmen. I was boxing for the Syracuse Boys Club Boxing Program. I went to the Main Street Gym on the 300 block of North Salina Street in Syracuse. This was where all the local fighters trained at that time. Carmen was boxing then, but was also working at a factory on Wolf Street. He would train after work. He would take time to work with me, and I learned a lot from Carmen. He was a people person, and sometimes things like that rub off on a young boy. He was always a fun guy to be with, but he also had a short fuse. If he got mad at somebody, he would let them know it. I've seen Carmen do that many a time, but Carmen is a great guy and a great guy for the sport of boxing. You talk about the American dream, here's a guy, he's ten years old, and he wants to be champion of the world. Some guys want to be president, but they don't become president. He did become champion. He's an amazing guy."

8. International Boxing Club directors. *(Left to right):* James Norris, Arthur Wirtz, and Truman Gibson. *Courtesy of Carmen Basilio.*

3.

The Formation of a Monster

in January 1949, associates of heavyweight champion Joe Louis visited Chicago businessman James D. Norris at his winter home in Coral Gables, Florida, regarding a proposal to promote heavyweight fights. Norris, the forty-one-year-old son of James P. Norris, the owner of the Detroit Red Wings National Hockey League team, had been on the fringe of boxing for the past fifteen years. Norris had dabbled in promoting a few fights in Chicago while owning a small percentage of a number of fighters. Together with his father and Arthur Wirtz, a successful Chicago real estate investor, they owned the Chicago Stadium, the St. Louis Arena, and the Detroit Olympia and had lease options on the Indianapolis Coliseum, the Omaha Coliseum, and the Cincinnati Gardens. They produced the profitable Hollywood Ice Revue while owning considerable stock in Madison Square Garden Corporation. Norris was also involved in horse racing, owning a stable of thoroughbred horses that he raced throughout the country. He was a very respected businessman of considerable wealth and social contacts.

Joe Louis had been the heavyweight champ since June 1937, when he knocked out James Braddock in Chicago. During his reign he had made tremendous amounts of money, but the government was now chasing him for back taxes in excess of a million dollars. The aging champion was nearing the end of a great career and wanted to retire, but he was forced to continue boxing because he needed money. He had recently completed a series of boxing exhibitions that had been organized by Harry Mendel, a boxing promoter from New Jersey. Mendel had been a close friend of Louis since the early 1930s. A short man with an engaging personality, Mendel told Louis he had just the plan that would allow Joe to retire from boxing but still have a vehicle in place to make huge amounts of money. The "Mendel Plan" had Joe Louis secure exclusive service contracts with the four top contenders for his heavyweight title. Once the fighters were under contract, Joe Louis would announce his retirement from boxing. Then, Louis through his company, Joe Louis Enterprises, Inc., would assign those contracts to a third party, who would have the right to promote world heavyweight bouts. Louis loved the plan and contacted his close friend and attorney Truman Gibson to get his opinion on what Mendel was proposing. Gibson had befriended Joe Louis in early 1942, when he was working as an assistant to the secretary of war, Henry L. Stimpson. Gibson had been put in charge of a proposed bout between Louis and Billy Conn that would benefit the Army Relief Fund. The fight went awry, but Gibson had gained some valuable experience and interest regarding the business of boxing, besides becoming acquainted with the heavyweight champion of the world.

Following World War II, Louis had asked Truman Gibson to help him with his tax problems that had recently surfaced. Gibson went about untangling Louis's tax mess, suggesting to him that he form Joe Louis Enterprises, Inc., which would ultimately help reduce his tax burden. A grateful Joe Louis was impressed. When Harry Mendel suggested his plan to Louis, Joe immediately called Gibson. The tall, highly respected lawyer quickly saw an opportunity to get involved in boxing. Gibson flew to Florida that night, expecting to represent Joe Louis at his first meeting with James Norris.

The next morning at breakfast, Harry Mendel told Louis and Gibson that it would be better for all concerned if he went by himself to meet with Norris. Mendel suggested to the two black men that Norris was expecting he to come by himself, and now having an attorney present may send the wrong message. Louis agreed. Truman Gibson was furious, believing it was a black-white issue because they were in the South, but he remained calm. The remainder of their meeting he quizzed Mendel about his idea.

Harry Mendel's meeting with James Norris went extremely well, and Norris arranged a second meeting in Chicago, with his partner, Arthur Wirtz. This time Mendel would be accompanied by Truman Gibson. Joe Louis instructed Harry Mendel before leaving for Chicago that Gibson would be representing all of them in this meeting. He would handle the negotiations from then on.

Arthur Wirtz was a shrewd businessman who complemented Jim Norris's entrepreneurial spirit. After graduating from the University of Michigan in 1922, Wirtz returned to Chicago, where he went into the real estate business. A workaholic, Wirtz prospered from the stock market crash, buying up distressed properties for pennies on the dollar. In the 1930s he became involved in sports, forming a partnership with Norris and his father to purchase a hockey team for Chicago. When their efforts failed in Chicago, they turned their attention to the Detroit hockey franchise that was for sale. In 1933 they bought the team and the arena, the Olympia, where the team played all its home games. Two years later Norris and Wirtz purchased the financially strapped Chicago Stadium, home to the Chicago Black Hawks. (In 1954 they would purchase the hockey team.)

Arthur Wirtz was a tall, imposing man with a gruff personality. He attentively listened to Truman Gibson lay out the plan that again revealed that Joe Louis would deliver the personal service contracts of the four top heavyweight fighters. The meeting hit a snag when Gibson said that Norris and Wirtz would be required to give Joe Louis $250,000 and 51 percent of the proposed company. Louis, Gibson also pointed out, would be very active in the day-to-day operation of the company.

Wirtz, sitting with his arms folded, stared at Gibson, shaking his head in disbelief, not pleased with the financial terms. Standing up, he thanked Gibson and Mendel for thinking of Norris and himself, but at that price they would have to pass. He encouraged Gibson to find another partner for their intriguing idea, because he thought that it had merit, but not at those prices. Gibson advised him that there were ongoing discussions with other people regarding this plan by Mendel, but he wanted Norris and Wirtz to be considered. Wirtz, handing Gibson his topcoat, said that he would speak with Norris about their plan by phone that night. If Norris wanted to pursue it, perhaps with some different terms, he would be happy to get together with them again. "If Jim says he wants to go forward with this, we will get back to you, but at the amount Mr. Louis wants, I can't see us moving forward. The numbers would have to change significantly before we would get involved. We both appreciate you thinking of us." Wirtz then escorted Gibson and Mendel out of his office.

A few days later Truman Gibson called Arthur Wirtz, offering to meet again, because he believed there was some common ground between the two parties that needed to be explored further. "Also," Gibson said, "Joe Louis has heard a great deal of good things about the two of you and wants you involved with this project." A third meeting was scheduled, this time with Jim Norris and Joe Louis present. Joe Louis, in need of money, had instructed Gibson prior to the meeting to get a deal done. Under no circumstances could they walk out of there with no agreement in place. Harry Mendel, the creator of the plan, was not included.

A frank discussion ensued, with the sharp legal mind of Truman Gibson tangling with the formidable negotiation skills of Arthur Wirtz. Gibson told Norris and Wirtz that although they could certainly work with others, they would prefer developing their plan with gentlemen with the business acumen that both of them possessed. It was confirmed during the meeting that the National Boxing Association (NBA) would sanction the winner of the proposed fight-off as heavyweight champion. Norris and Wirtz both smiled at that revelation. Joe Louis reaffirmed to them that he had verbal agreements with the four top contenders: Ezzard Charles, Jersey Joe Walcott, Lou Savold, and Gus Lesnevich.

After some give-and-take on both sides, it was agreed that Louis would be paid $150,000 and 20 percent of the proposed stock. He was to be advanced $15,000, which was to be used to bind Savold and Lesnevich. It was also agreed that this meeting would remain secret. First, Joe Louis was still legally tied to Mike Jacobs, the top fight promoter in New York, who had two years remaining on an exclusive contract with Madison Square Garden. The high-strung Jacobs had recently suffered a stroke and was in forced semiretirement. Gibson was confident that all contracts could be disavowed because of the state of Jacobs's health. Second, Louis needed to get the four contenders under personal service contracts, which included the rights to radio, television, and movie revenues. Once Louis had each of the four contenders signed, their contracts would be assigned to the newly formed International Boxing Clubs with James D. Norris as president.

Joe Louis, with the help of Truman Gibson, quickly secured the contracts of the four top heavyweight fighters. Next, Mike Jacobs was bought out of his contracts for $100,000. The International Boxing Clubs of Illinois and New York were now officially in business. In a span of a little more than four months, James Norris had gained exclusive control of the heavyweight divisions of boxing, besides controlling the top arenas in four major cities in the United States. He was being hailed by the press as someone who would be good for boxing. He was a true sportsman, a person in it for the love of the game. He would change the face of boxing. Unfortunately, that face would be a far cry from what people imagined.

9. *(Left to right):* Joe Nitro, Carmen Basilio, and John DeJohn. *Courtesy of Carmen Basilio.*

4.

Getting Down to Business

the Winter Olympic Games in 1952 were held in Helsinki, Finland, under added world pressure. The Korean conflict raged on, as attempts at a truce failed. The Soviet Union, entering the Games for the first time since 1912, decided to house all the Eastern-bloc athletes away from the Olympic Village, at a nearby Russian naval base. Each day the athletes would be chauffeured to and from the Games after completing their competitions, eliminating any social contact with athletes from the United States and Europe. This action only added fuel to the cold war, creating an "East versus West" mentality. The competition was intense. An American figure skater, Dick Button, took home the gold medal, having perfecting the "double axel" just days before the competition began.

In November 1952, Dwight Eisenhower would defeat Adlai Stevenson to become the nation's thirty-fourth president. The highlight of the campaign was the Checkers speech of Eisenhower's running mate, Richard Nixon. The nation saw an emotional candidate on September 23, 1952, respond to charges that he had misused political funds. His impassioned plea to the American people was that he would never do anything so dishonest as to be a part of a secret political slush fund. Everything he did was aboveboard, and he could be trusted. He portrayed himself as a victim of low-class politics by the Democrats. He vowed never to return a dog named Checkers that was sent to his family as a gift. This cleverly conceived speech played well with voters, which ensured his position on the Republican ticket, thereby salvaging his political career.

A new crop of fighters was moving onto the scene in 1952, slowly pushing aside some of the great champions of the past. Young fighters such as Rocky Marciano, Randy Turpin, and Bobo Olsen joined Sugar Ray Robinson, Ezzard Charles, and Jersey Joe Walcott as the new face of boxing. Joe Louis, Willie Pep, Rocky Graziano, and Jake La Motta were all beginning to show signs that they had stayed too long at the fair. These new young guns had a future, and they had direction, a vision of what they wanted to do. The old pugs had memories of great pasts mixed with unrealistic hopes of what lay ahead. The fighters that they once were no longer showed up at the arena, and they began to lose battles that a few years before they would have won. You get no victories in boxing for what you did yesterday. The piper always gets paid.

Carmen Basilio entered 1952 unsure of his career as a professional boxer. Five losses in the previous eight fights had shaken his confidence. He was at a point where he started to question whether a career as a professional fighter was worth all his time and effort. Perhaps his mother was right, and he should get out of this dirty, rotten game. His dream of becoming a champion began to seem further away each day. He was making little money and was getting nowhere. One step forward, two steps back. He lost his last fight, in New Orleans in September 1951, to a guy named Ross Virgo. Something had to change, or it was time to hang it up.

CARMEN BASILIO: "The past couple of years I had been working with the Amos brothers. I had quite a few fights with them. It became clear that I wasn't going anyplace with them. They became greedy. They didn't care about me. All they were interested in was the money. They weren't coming to the gym. They weren't teaching me anything. I was going to the gym by myself and all that. They never came around anymore."

DICKIE DIVERONICA (Boxer): "Carmen was getting no management in the early 1950s. These two brothers didn't care a lick about him. They would throw him in with experienced fighters. They didn't care. He wasn't ready yet for that type of competition.

Carmen would fight anybody. That is why he had a number of losses to guys he would have destroyed a few years later."

In addition to poor management Basilio had become sick with mononucleosis in mid-1950. Refusing to take time off to properly rest, his health was an issue in his lackluster performances throughout the last half of 1950 and during the entire year of 1951.

GREG SORRENTINO (Boxer): "Talk about terrible stuff. He drove down to New Orleans to fight Ross Virgo for seven hundred bucks. He broke his hand, which cost him the fight. Besides having mono, with the lymph nodes under his arms the size of golf balls, he ran into a blizzard on the way back driving on Route 11. The window in the car was broken, his hand was broken . . . all for a lousy seven hundred dollars. His take was 30 percent, with the rest going to his managers. So what did he end up with? He couldn't fight, and he couldn't work. He had to put a big, oversized glove over his broken hand so he could make fifty cents an hour shoveling sidewalks for the City of Syracuse. I mean, if that's not hunger . . . He deserved to make it because he made himself make it."

Early in 1952, Carmen Basilio began working with John DeJohn and Joe Nitro. The thirty-eight-year-old DeJohn, from Syracuse, was the oldest of seven boys. Five of his brothers were professional boxers, with Mike a heavyweight and Joey a middleweight still fighting at that time. His brother Ralph fought in the 1930s and 1940s, before injuries shortened his career. A power puncher, he fought five world champions during a solid professional career.

JOHN DEJOHN: "I was the only one who didn't fight. Oh, I was tough in street fights, but I felt that being the oldest, I had a greater responsibility. I made sure my brothers were taken care of. We were born into fighting. My father never fought, but he was a laborer and as strong as they come. I saw him dump a few guys when he had to. Nobody with any sense messed with my old man."

Joe Nitro had been around boxing since he was sixteen years old, dating back to the early 1920s. Syracuse promoter Tommy Ryan hired him to handle odd jobs for him, starting out as a call boy who was responsible for advising fighters when it was their

10. Joe Nitro in the 1920s with one of his fighters, Jess Doctor. *Courtesy of Carmen Basilio.*

time to go in the ring. Nitro became friendly with the boxers, fight managers, and trainers who came through Syracuse. Soon Ryan expanded his role to matching up boxers for his preliminaries. A renowned cheapskate, Ryan had trouble signing up fighters for the few dollars he would pay them. Nitro would scour the Syracuse area for fighters. He would go into the Italian, Irish, German, and Polish neighborhoods, uncovering some outstanding hometown talent. Because neighborhood rivalries were so intense at that time, the preliminary matches were as big a drawing card as the main events. Nitro eventually began to manage fighters, building a solid stable of fighters in the late 1920s. Later he managed Ralph, Mike, and Joey DeJohn. Nitro commuted to Syracuse from

Ithaca, staying at the Wood Hotel in downtown Syracuse. A whiz at numbers and statistics, when he wasn't studying boxing he was playing the horses—a habit that sometimes left him short on dough.

CARMEN BASILIO: "Joe Nitro was an okay guy, but he gambled on the horses and gave all his money to the bookies."

DONNIE HAMILTON (Boxing Historian): "During the war Joe went to work for the Ithaca Gun Company. My uncle had also worked there during that time. Years later I asked him if he knew Joe Nitro. He said that he knew him but not too well because he hid in the back with a horse sheet. He said he did very little work because he was always studying the horse sheets."

John DeJohn approached Basilio with a plan of action to get his career back on track. DeJohn would become his trainer, and Joe Nitro would assist him, doubling as Basilio's business manager. Nitro would handle all the public relations, sending out information about Carmen to newspapers and promoters, making sure that his name was out there. The three men formed a partnership that lasted the remainder of Carmen Basilio's career.

CARMEN BASILIO: "I was still working my day job when I met DeJohn and Nitro. I told them, 'If you rob me, you rob yourself, because I will quit fighting. Don't rob me and I won't rob you.'"

Carmen Basilio, working under the guidance of his new team, started to win, defeating three straight opponents. Always in great physical shape, Basilio under DeJohn's watchful eye sharpened his boxing skills. Each day in the gym they would work on his footwork, with the emphasis on Basilio keeping his feet balanced, staying on the balls of his feet so that he could better attack his opponent. Basilio would practice moving from side to side, learning to shift and shuffle his feet quickly, keeping them close to the ground so he always had a solid base under him. He worked on improving his punching techniques, learning to deliver better combinations instead of wildly attacking his opponent. He began throwing short punches, aimed at an area no bigger than the size of a basketball. He refined all his punches so that now they became more effective. He increased the power of his left cross by rotating his hips and

11. Carmen Basilio in training.
Courtesy of Carmen Basilio.

torso counterclockwise as the punch was delivered. He learned to throw the punch from his chin, focusing on a straight-line approach to the target. The left shoulder was thrust forward and finished just touching outside the chin, while his right hand was tucked back to protect his face.

The Basilio hook that later destroyed Tony DeMarco and Johnny Saxton was a semicircular punch that Carmen threw with either hand. He worked on bringing his elbow back with a horizontal fist with the knuckles pointing forward. The rear hand was always placed by the jaw to protect the chin. He learned to pivot his lead foot clockwise as the punch was thrown, turning the right heel outward, while again rotating his hips and torso. He worked over and over on refining these important fundamentals. Adding better boxing skills to a fighter with the heart of a lion made him a very dangerous opponent. He was now prepared to match up with some of the better welterweights, beginning with Chuck Davey.

DONNIE HAMILTON (Boxing Historian): "Johnny DeJohn made Carmen a good fighter. Before Carmen met Johnny, he used to go up to the gym every day after work and train. Nobody was showing him nothing. I would see him up there day after day, training by himself. I never saw the Amos brothers at the gym. I mean never. You would think they would have come around once in a while. Never. When Tony, the oldest Amos brother, died, that's when Johnny and Joe took over. Johnny learned a lot about boxing from his brother Ralph, who had fought five world champions in the 1930s. He was a hell of a fighter. Ralph knew how to train boxers, and Johnny learned from him. Johnny never boxed, but he knew the sport. He made some moves that benefited Carmen. If Carmen was the king, then Johnny was the kingmaker. Johnny was shrewd, and he learned how to deal with people."

GREG SORRENTINO (Boxer): "Johnny DeJohn was a boxing genius. I worked and was around guys like Angelo Dundee, Eddie Futch, and Emmanuel Stuart, but nobody but nobody taught me any more than Johnny did. He was very wise; he studied the sport. He knew the angles and dropping the hook. He would say boxing is like meshing gears. Anybody can make somebody miss by six, eight inches, but if you make somebody miss by half an inch, you are right there to counterpunch. Here was a guy that never left Syracuse but was one of the best trainers of all time. Johnny, he studied the sport and made his living with the sport that was his living. He was a fight manager, and he did very well with it. Carmen went through managers—he had lots of different ones—and he didn't go anywhere until he hooked up with Johnny. I think DeJohn recognized something in Carmen. Remember that all the DeJohn brothers were good fighters, main-event fighters. I think that hooking up with him raised Carmen's game to a different level.

Johnny and Joe [Nitro] were able to take those raw ingredients and develop them a little bit farther down the line than some of those earlier managers of Carmen could. Johnny became a wealthy man because of Carmen, not because of his brothers. I mean, he made a living because of his brothers but became rich with Carmen."

Chuck Davey, the handsome former National Collegiate Athletic Association featherweight champion, was a slick boxer who fought as a southpaw. He had become a very popular fighter on television, and the prevailing opinion was that International Boxing Club president Jim Norris was grooming the Irish welterweight for a match with then welterweight champion Kid Gavilan. Norris wanted Davey to have a few more fights under his belt before challenging Gavilan, beginning with Carmen Basilio. Their fight had originally been scheduled to be fought in Syracuse, in early April 1952, but was rescheduled twice to allow a supposed cut Davey suffered during training to heal. Finally, on May 29, 1952, the two aspiring welterweights met.

Basilio gained the early advantage in the match with his aggressive style of fighting, keeping the pressure on Davey throughout each round. Davey took a lot of punishment but rallied in the later rounds, scoring with a series of jabs, hooks, and uppercuts. When they went to the scorecards following the match, it was determined that Basilio had won a close decision. A recount was demanded by Davey and the IBC, and a few days later the fight was ruled a draw.

DONNIE HAMILTON (Boxing Historian): "When Carmen fought Chuck Davey it was a hell of a fight. Three things happened. Joe Palmer was the referee for the fight. Also, it was Carmen's first main-event fight under the promotion of Norm Rothschild. The Davey people wanted to get out of the fight after they signed for it. Norm said no. Johnny DeJohn said we want to fight this guy, so they held them to it. That was probably the biggest crowd up to that time that Carmen ever fought before. Carmen went after him, busting him over both eyes. In the tenth round, Joe Palmer stops the fight. He took Davey over to Dr. Heck, and he let the fight continue. When the final bell rang Carmen got a split decision. That night he won the fight. Four days later they found a mistake on Joe Palmer's addition, so they ended up throwing his scorecard out and called it a draw. The great thing about it was it went over all the major wire services. That was a first for Carmen."

The overturn of the decision forced a second match six weeks later in Chicago. Davey went into this nationally televised bout a 4-1 favorite. This time around Davey came out fast, outboxing his opponent in the early rounds, but Basilio rallied back and had Davey in trouble in both the ninth and the tenth rounds. Basilio attacked Davey with a barrage of punches that opened nasty cuts under both eyes. He relentlessly kept up the attack but couldn't put Davey away. When the scorecards were added up, Davey was given a unanimous decision. Basilio and his handlers were furious about the results.

CARMEN BASILIO: "It was a lousy house decision. If this fight was fought anywhere else they would have stopped it. It's nice when you're on the right side. The IBC side. He can't fight. Fast but no punch. They watched him like a mother hen watching chicks. He couldn't lose . . . not here. I want a rematch, but I ain't got much chance of getting one."

CHUCK DAVEY (Boxer): "I thought I started faster in this match than I did in Syracuse. He butted me and the blood blinded me in the ninth so I couldn't see the punches coming at all."

There was a crowd of 4,093 who paid a gross gate of $12,800. Each fighter was paid $3,469.28 and the standard fee of $1,500 for television. The two fighters could have drawn 8,000-plus in Syracuse, but to the chagrin of local Syracuse promoter Norm Rothschild, the fight had gone west to the Windy City.

NORM ROTHSCHILD (Syracuse Promoter): "Basilio's team [DeJohn and Nitro] apparently wanted to stay in good graces with the IBC, by staging the fight in Chicago. They passed up a big payday by not having the fight here. It doesn't sound like a good business decision to me. I sincerely hope Carmen can stay in the so-called TV big-time. But when he loses a few times and is dropped by the IBC, he surely will be out of the big money in Syracuse."

12. Program cover featuring Kid Gavilan and Carmen Basilio, 1953. *Courtesy of Carmen Basilio.*

5.

A Sugar Meltdown and the "Keed" Comes to Town

light heavyweight champion Joey Maxim was born Giuseppe Antonio Berardinelli on March 28, 1922. Never known as a power puncher, his slick style of boxing was more reminiscent of the rat-a-tat-tat of a machine gun firing. When he turned professional, he cleverly took the name Maxim, after the Maxim machine gun. A solid boxer with a granite chin, Maxim became the lightweight champion in 1950, with a surprise knockout of British title holder Freddie Mills. After the fight it was discovered that three of Mills's teeth were embedded in Maxim's glove. In the first defense of his title, he beat Irish Bob Murphy in August 1951.

Maxim's second title defense would be against Sugar Ray Robinson at Yankee Stadium on June 25, 1952. Robinson, the reigning middleweight champion, had knocked out the aging Rocky Graziano in three rounds in Chicago two months before. Sugar Ray was looking to add the light heavyweight title to his résumé. In Maxim he had an opponent who was slower, lacked the boxing skills he possessed, and wasn't a power puncher. Everything pointed to a Robinson victory.

Sugar Ray went into the fight a 13-10 favorite and, as expected, dominated the fight through the first ten rounds, beating the slower Maxim to the punch. Expending huge amounts of energy, the one hundred–degree heat began to take its toll on Sugar Ray as the fight reached its later stages. The conditions became so unbearable that veteran referee Ruby Goldstein had to be replaced in the tenth round, succumbing to the heat and humidity. In the thirteenth round Robinson was clearly in trouble, falling to the canvas in exhaustion after missing a punch. His handlers had to drag his limp body to his corner following the round. Ring physician Dr. Alexander Schiff quickly jumped into the ring to examine Robinson. When he asked the exhausted fighter if he could continue, Sugar Ray shook his head and said, "I'm done." Joey Maxim had won by doing less. The fight was scored a TKO.

ARTHUR DALEY (Writer): "There was an air of unreality to the entire fight. Joey Maxim did nothing and won the fight. Sugar Ray Robinson did everything and lost it. Perhaps Robinson, a proud and vain man, became too enamored with his own magnificence. The artistry of the Harlem millionaire was positively breathtaking. He hit Maxim at will, manhandled him and exposed him for the mediocrity he must be."

JOEY MAXIM (Boxer): "Robinson's punches began losing steam in the eleventh. I knew he was getting ready to go. If he had come out in the fourteenth, I would have knocked him out."

SUGAR RAY ROBINSON (Boxer): "I lasted longer than Goldstein, and nobody was hitting him. Maxim didn't beat me . . . God did."

Following the fight, Maxim's manager, Doc Kearns, protected his fighter's reputation, saying it was all about winning, being the last man standing. He reminded everyone that it was just as hot for Maxim as it was for Robinson.

●   ●   ●

Kid Gavilan was born Gerardo Gonzalez on January 6, 1926, in Palo Seco, Cuba. When he was three years old his family moved to the port city Camagüey, where his parents found work harvesting sugar cane. Laboring in the fields six days a week, his mother and father dealt with an unforgiving sun, poisonous snakes, and poor wages. Each day they were paid by the amount of cane they harvested, barely carving out a living.

When he was ten years old, Gerardo began to hang out at the local boxing gym, which was near where he lived in Camagüey. Each day he would go and watch the local fighters work out, intrigued by these men and impressed by how hard they worked. When his mother became aware of where her young son was spending his time, Mama Gonzales was angry. She forbade him from going back to that terrible place, telling him that he was old enough to begin helping them in the fields. Gerardo pleaded with his mother to let him box, explaining to her that his hands were for boxing, not cutting sugar cane. He promised her that he would make her proud. He would become the champion of Cuba. She adored her little boy and reluctantly agreed. This way she would at least know where he was.

In 1943, when he was seventeen years old, Gerardo turned professional, winning his first match, a four-round decision in Havana. He proceeded to win nine more fights, with one bout scored a draw. His obvious talent caught the eye of a Havana café owner, Fernando do Bailed, who dubbed him "El Gavilan," which means "The Hawk." Yamil Chade, a local businessman, became Kid Gavilan's manager. Chade, with little background in boxing, saw a business opportunity with this young prodigy and took control of his career. In 1946, Chade decided to bring Gavilan to the United States to see how his young fighter stacked up against American boxers. After Gavilan convincingly won three straight matches, Chide knew he had something special. They returned to Cuba for a brief holiday, then it was back in the gym for more intense training.

In September 1947, Kid Gavilan came back to the United States to stay. His exciting boxing style quickly caught the attention of fight fans on the East Coast. He soon began to draw comparisons to "Kid Chocolate," a great Cuban fighter from the 1930s. "Kid Chocolate," Eligio Sardinias Montalbo, was Cuba's first champion, winning the junior lightweight title in 1931. He combined a very stylish boxing technique with outstanding punching power. Gavilan, although not known for his punching power, gained notoriety for his bolo punch. It was a combination of a looping uppercut and a right cross, delivered from below the knees. Although he is credited in many circles for creating the bolo punch, there were other fighters before him who used a similar-looking punch, but none had the grace or ability of Kid Gavilan.

In early 1948, Gavilan fought lightweight champion Ike Williams, losing a tough ten-round decision. Posting four more wins, he got a date with then welterweight champion Sugar Ray Robinson. In a nontitle fight, Robinson bested Gavilan over ten tough rounds. Robinson had respect for Gavilan's talent, and his training schedule reflected it. Each fighter rocked one another with hard punches, but the more complete fighter, Sugar Ray Robinson, won out in the end.

Kid Gavilan put together another streak of wins, defeating seven straight opponents, including avenging his loss to Ike Williams, beating him twice in early 1949. This set up a repeat match with Sugar Ray Robinson, this time with the welterweight title at stake. On July 11, 1949, they fought in Philadelphia, again with the same result, Robinson winning a unanimous decision. Sugar Ray had nothing but praise for his opponent.

SUGAR RAY ROBINSON (Boxer): "He not only was aggressive, but you could hit him with everything and still not knock him out. He is a very good fighter."

The Cuban fighter remained busy over the next two years, fighting twenty-five times, winning nineteen. During that time he had wins over Beau Jack, Laurent Dauthuille, and Joe Miceli and split two fights with Billy Graham.

On May 18, 1951, he was chosen to fight Johnny Bratton for the welterweight crown that became vacated when Robinson moved up as middleweight champion. Gavilan, primed for his chance at a world title, had Bratton in trouble from the first round, coasting to an easy victory.

ARTHUR DALEY (Writer): "The Kid did an awesome job on Johnny Bratton, the house fighter for Octopus Incorporated (IBC). The Cuban hotshot is a beautiful boxer and a great television favorite. His style is ordinarily just as sporadic. Gavilan will let go with a furious flurry, almost like a madman gone berserk. Then he'll coast. Then, with a quick peek at the clock, he'll time his closing sprint just before the end of each round with the hope of convincing the ring officials that he's delivered that identical kind of fisticuffing for the entire three minutes. Even the least gullible of them sometimes find it difficult to disregard the psychological seed he's planted especially in a close round."

Leading into 1953, Gavilan had successfully defended his title four times, beating Billy Graham twice in New York. Their first fight was a Mob-influenced fight, where he benefited from an unfair decision. Gavilan soundly beat Graham in their rematch nine months later, proving he could beat Graham without anyone's help.

CHICO VEJAR (Boxer): "Kid Gavilan was very busy during a fight. When you did something to get an edge against him, he always seemed to have a way to neutralize it. He was a fan's fighter. He was very flashy, very colorful."

JOE MICELI (Boxer): "Gavilan was great. He was a real showman. He was very cute in the ring. The crowd liked him. He did things in the ring long before Muhammad Ali came along."

On February 11, 1953, Chuck Davey finally got his shot at the crown and Kid Gavilan. The IBC-sponsored title match was fought in Chicago, on national television. Gavilan dominated the fight from the start, scoring a TKO over Davey in the tenth round. By knocking out the popular Irishman, the Hawk eliminated any decision from being placed in the hands of the IBC-selected judges.

KID GAVILAN (Boxer): "I no in trouble anytime. He no hard puncher and I know I have him after the first time I knock him down."

Following the fight Gavilan talked of moving up to the middleweight division, but that idea was put on hold. It was decided that Gavilan would fight a series of nontitle bouts throughout the summer of 1953. The next defense of his championship would be against the onion picker from Canastota. The site would be Carmen Basilio's backyard, Syracuse, New York.

John DeJohn was summoned to New York in the summer of 1953 to have lunch with Frankie Carbo. Arriving at the Warwick Hotel, DeJohn was surprised that Angel Lopez, Kid Gavilan's trainer, was seated next to Carbo. On the trip to New York, DeJohn kept going over in his mind what Carbo wanted to see him about. All he knew was that Carbo had said it would be very worthwhile for the two of them to get together. DeJohn wasn't sure if it involved Carmen Basilio or one of his two brothers. Carbo had been a bit evasive on the telephone about why he wanted to get together. DeJohn, seeing Lopez sitting there, knew now why Carbo wanted to see him. He was thinking of matching Basilio up against the welterweight champion.

Fighting Gavilan at that particular time was not a match DeJohn wanted. Basilio was becoming a very good fighter under DeJohn's guidance, showing daily improvement, but DeJohn didn't think Carmen was quite ready for a fighter of the champion's caliber. The last thing he wanted to do was rush Basilio. There was such an upside to this kid that there was no need yet to be fighting for titles. He knew Basilio didn't think that way—hell, that's all he talked about . . . getting a title shot, making his dreams come true.

Frankie Carbo's plan was simple: he wanted to get Basilio away from Ray Arcel, who was in competition with the IBC, promoting boxing on television. The bait would be a shot at the welterweight crown, fought in Basilio's backyard, Syracuse, New York. Carbo knew that Basilio didn't like the IBC because of the Davey fight, and he had heard Basilio didn't like him. Carbo could not care less what a fighter's opinion of him was. This was about making money.

"Look, John, if you let Basilio fight Gavilan, you guys will make more money than you have ever made before," Carbo began.

"What do you mean by a lot of money?"

Carbo smiled, then reached into his coat pocket and took out a piece of paper. "John, the standard rate for a challenger in a championship fight is 20 percent. The champion gets 40 percent. Everybody knows that. You know that you will draw a lot of money in Syracuse, which means you will make more than you have ever earned. It's a simple supply and demand. Let me ask you, how many title fights have they had in Syracuse? I have a feeling this might be the first one, and if you win . . . you guys are going to make a lot more money. Now, before you say anything, I asked Angel here today to show that he's on board with this and that I want this to happen in September in Syracuse. Are you with us?"

John DeJohn was hooked. He knew Basilio wanted the fight but would not be happy if he knew Carbo put it together. DeJohn told Carbo that they had a deal.

DICKIE DiVERONICA (Boxer): "John DeJohn had to deal with the Mob guys. That's the way business was conducted in those days. Carmen, he never had any dealings with those guys. He didn't want anything to do with them."

Carmen Basilio had had a very busy fourteen months since his bitter loss to Chuck Davey. Basilio had fought nine times, which included three tough matches with Billy Graham. After losing to Graham by decision in Chicago in August 1952, he beat "Brawling Billy" in a donnybrook in Syracuse for the New York welterweight title. Weeks later they did it again in Syracuse, with this one scored a draw. Basilio also fought during that stretch Ike Williams, winning a convincing match over the veteran boxer in January 1953. Basilio attacked Williams throughout the fight with a heavy dose of body blows, piling up points round after round. In the fourth round the two fighters bumped heads, with Basilio suffering a cut over his eye. Angelo Dundee, Carmen's outstanding cutman, patched him up between rounds, and the injury was not a problem for the remainder of the fight. Basilio won a unanimous decision.

IKE WILLIAMS: "Basilio's a good fighter, with a great future. He can take a punch. I hit him with some great shots, but he took them and kept on coming."

CARMEN BASILIO: "Ike is the hardest puncher I have faced. I got in close and he hit me two shots in my forearms that picked me off my feet. I said to myself he's not going to hit me again and he didn't thank goodness. Ike's a tough guy."

DONNIE HAMILTON (Boxing Historian): "What turned Carmen around was when he fought Billy Graham in Chicago. Graham beat him decisively, but he learned from that fight how to get past the jab. If you look at his record after that, he lost very few fights from then on. He just kept improving."

All the prefight talk leading into the Basilio-Gavilan bout focused on whether the champion could hold off the aggressive style of the challenger. Gavilan scoffed at such talk, saying there was no way that Basilio would overpower him. He breezed through his last hard workout prior to the fight, sparring five rounds. During the sparring session he treated the spectators to a show, waltzing around the ring with his hands at his side, bobbing and weaving, yapping at his young sparring partner as he tried to hit him. Each time his sparring mate missed, Gavilan attacked him with a series of lightning-quick punches. Occasionally, he would fake throwing his famous bolo punch, accompanied by considerable clowning. When he was done sparring, he shadowboxed around the gym, shuffling up close to an unsuspecting fan, letting go with a flurry of combinations that would come within a quarter-inch of their nose. He had everyone laughing as he selected victim after victim. "The Keed" seemed confident and ready to defend his title.

At the Basilio camp the mood was much more serious as Johnny DeJohn and Joe Nitro put their guy through his final workout. Building confidence was the focus as Basilio closed out his training for his first world title championship fight. Carmen had become a different fighter under their tutelage. They could see the daily improvement, day by day, match by match. They were now fighting the best fighters in the world—in important matches. The mental aspect was as important as knowing how to throw a left hook.

JOE NITRO (Trainer): "This boy is great. He's just got to learn one thing, when to punch and when to take it easy. This boy will out punch that fellow and he will hurt him too. This fellow will make that champion give ground. All he has to do is remember not to waste himself."

WHITEY LEWIS (Writer): "Carmen Basilio is a rough fighter who pitches his fists from second base as well as from left field and from the back of the plate. He is gifted with abnormal endurance. Not a puncher who can flatten a man with one terrifying blow, he still has enough power to stretch out unwary foes. He hits often enough to make up for any lack of killer force."

CARMEN BASILIO: "I feel great. I'm going to be the next welterweight champion of the world. Believe me. I'm going to be the next champion. It's a dream I've had for a long time. Nothing is going to get in my way."

•   •   •

SYRACUSE, NEW YORK, SEPTEMBER 18, 1953. Kid Gavilan, in the sixth defense of his title, entered the ring a 4-1 favorite to retain his crown. The first world championship fight ever to be staged at the Onondaga County War Memorial attracted more than seventy-five hundred screaming fans who were treated to a torrid battle.

Kid Gavilan, as was his style, came out strong, scoring with effective jabs to Carmen Basilio's face, causing some puffiness and discoloration around his left eye. In the second round the champion kept using his right jab, whap-whap-whap, continually hitting Basilio in the face. The challenger kept moving forward, taking punch after punch, trying to get inside. Finally, feinting with his right, Basilio moved under Gavilan's jab and caught him with a left hook, knocking him to the canvas. Clearly shaken by the force of the blow, the champion was up at the count of eight. Still woozy, Gavilan used all his knowledgeable ring skills to survive the round. Basilio kept the pressure on the unsteady Gavilan through the next four rounds, but he could not put the champion away. In the seventh round the fight started to change, as Gavilan became more confident and began to outbox Basilio, this time staying out of range of Carmen's left hand. It was clear to Gavilan that any fighting inside favored the stronger, more aggressive Basilio, so he utilized his right jab, careful not to let the fight turn into a brawl. In the fifteenth round, Basilio attacked Gavilan as the War Memorial crowd cheered him on, trying to will their man on to victory. When the bell sounded to end the fight, the place was in a complete uproar. Each fighter had fought hard, and now it was up to the judges and referee to decide who would get the title.

While the chant "Basilio, Basilio, Basilio" echoed throughout the Onondaga County War Memorial, the votes were tabulated. Judge Harold Barnes voted seven rounds to six with two even . . . Gavilan. The other judge, Jim Kimball, had it seven rounds to five, with three even . . . Basilio. It was now left to referee George Walsh to determine who would be the victor. There was a quietness in the building as it was announced that Walsh had voted eight rounds to six with one even, the winner, and still welterweight champion of the world, Kid Gavilan.

For an instant after the decision was announced, there was an eerie silence in the Onondaga County War Memorial, a calm before the storm as Basilio fans came to grips with what they had just heard. The results were incongruent with what they had just witnessed, or what they thought they had just witnessed. Their man had fought hard, even knocking the champion down. That should have been enough. If one judge could see it Basilio's way, then surely one of the other two could see it his way too. Referee Walsh had been in the ring with the two fighters. What was he thinking? He could have voted for Carmen. A chair was tossed in the direction of the ring, which kicked off a torrent of booing and verbal abuse toward the referee. The security staff quickly formed a human chain around Walsh and escorted him out of the arena. He was pelted with beer cans and screams of outrage. Kid Gavilan's handlers, aware of the unruly crowd, had their fighter exit quickly, as he too was verbally chastised on his way to his dressing room. The Basilio camp, clearly upset by the verdict, was united in its support of its fighter and his future.

JOHN DEJOHN: "I thought Carmen won the fight. He was the aggressor all night. We have been on the short end lately . . . but that is going to change."

CARMEN BASILIO: "I was sure that I won that fight. To tell you the truth, I was so sure that I had won that I started to pace myself in the tenth round. I just didn't think that the fellow could beat me. Honestly, it wasn't a tough fight. He hit me with a few good shots but he never hit me as hard as some of the fellows I been fighting lately. I believe I deserve a rematch and I think they will have to give me one."

KID GAVILAN: "Basilio was a much tougher fighter than I expected. However, I think I beat him easily. After the first knockdown he never did anything else to me. But the crowd . . . they yell every time he throw a punch and it make me look bad."

DONNIE HAMILTON (Boxing Historian): "The Gavilan fight was a very close fight, but I honestly thought Carmen licked him. What hurt Carmen in that fight was he had a closed eye. They always talk about the closed eye in the Robinson fight. He had a closed eye in the Gavilan fight. Gavilan wasn't busted up, and that has a tendency to affect the judges. It could have gone either way. Also, that was Carmen's first fifteen-round fight. What he did not want to do going into the fight was punch himself out. He wanted to have enough gas at the end. He didn't know what it took to go fifteen rounds. He had Gavilan, and he let him off the hook."

In the dressing room an hour after the fight, Joe Nitro walked over to Basilio and knelt down to console his fighter, who was sitting alone with a towel over his head. "We'll get him next time, Carmen."

"You're damned right we will," Basilio replied.

Carmen Basilio never did get his rematch with Kid Gavilan. He would have to wait two years before getting another chance at the welterweight crown. He'd wait. Next time he would make sure it didn't go to a decision. He would take care of business before that happened.

DONNIE HAMILTON (Boxing Historian): "There was this guy Henny Andrews who was a promoter and manager in the Syracuse area. He at one time handled a fighter by the name of Nick Barone, who was a tough guy with a granite chin. When the Gavilan fight was about to happen, Norm [Rothschild] wanted to promote it. It was his dream to promote a championship bout. Norm had developed a good reputation with people in boxing, including the New York people [Gabe Genovese and Frankie Carbo]. By the time the fight came off in 1953, Henny Andrews was pretty much out of it. He wasn't promoting anymore. The New York people wanted eight hundred dollars to go to Henny Andrews. Norm didn't like Andrews, so I don't believe it went directly to Andrews from Norm. Anyway, Henny ended up with a check for eight hundred dollars. Later, he was downtown bragging that he promoted the fight, showing people this eight hundred–dollar check. Well, it got back to Norm, and he called the people in New York and said, 'You see what I mean about this guy?' They told Norm, 'Don't worry, he will never pass that check around again. We will take care of it.' After that you never heard another word about it."

ADA ROTHSCHILD (Wife): "Blinky Palermo was sitting next to me at the Gavilan fight. I didn't even know who he was. The commission at first wasn't going to let him attend the fight as a spectator, but then they decided he could. He was amazingly calm during the fight, and I remember he had a button missing off his coat. He didn't look like no Mafia guy to me."

●   ●   ●

Sugar Ray Robinson announced at the end of 1952 that he was stepping away from boxing. The Maxim fight had taken a toll on his body, and he wanted to pursue a career in show business while managing his various businesses. The greatest boxer of his era was stepping away after twelve years in professional boxing. The years of training and the constant physical abuse a boxer endures convinced him it was time to leave. The dehydration he had suffered from the heat and humidity in June had almost been fatal to him. It was two days before his body could handle solid foods, and it took him an abnormally long time to get his strength back. He would give up his middleweight crown for a pair of tap shoes and embark on a new way to entertain people, onstage instead of in a boxing ring. It was the right time to go. He was rich and famous, and, most important to Sugar Ray, he still had his health.

A four-man elimination tournament was arranged to determine who would become the new middleweight champion. Randy Turpin, Charlie Humez, Bobo Olsen, and Paddy Young were chosen to fight for the title. Turpin would fight Humez, while Olsen would square off against Young in the other semifinal match. The two winners would then meet to decide who would wear the belt. Sadly, one name was missing: Dave Sands.

Sands, possibly the best middleweight fighter in the early 1950s (this side of Sugar Ray Robinson), was critically injured on August 11, 1952, when a truck he was riding in overturned while he was at home in his native Australia. Sands later died in the hospital of internal injuries, leaving behind a pregnant wife, two daughters, and a son. His third daughter was born three months after his death.

Sands was the fifth of eight children born to a rough-and-tumble timber cutter from Burnt Bridge, Australia, George Ritchie. His family, of Aboriginal and European descent, were all very athletic people. His father was a boxer as well as a part-time rodeo rider. Dave's brothers, Clement, Percival, George, Alfred, and Russell, all boxed, emulating their father and great-uncle Bailey Russell, who was a bare-knuckle champion in Australia at the turn of the century. The brothers took the name Sands after a train conductor helped the boys out when traveling home after a series of boxing matches. It has been estimated that the Sands brothers fought in more than six hundred bouts over their careers. All very personable outside the ring, they are still considered Australia's greatest sporting family.

Dave Sands was by far the most gifted boxer in his family. He was very quick, an above-average counterpuncher, with power in each hand. His very aggressive fighting style and rock-hard chin had most overseas writers and commentators believing that he could compete with the top American fighters. During his career Sands won the Australian middleweight, light heavyweight, and heavyweight crowns.

13. The fighting Sands Brothers. Dave Sands is fourth from left.
Courtesy of Gary Youmans.

In March 1950, Sands fought Bobo Olsen, winning a close decision. He continued to post wins and was considered as an opponent against Sugar Ray Robinson in London in July 1951. Robinson, completing his European tour, considered fighting the Australian fighter. After a series of offers and counteroffers, Robinson decided against fighting Sands, instead choosing what was perceived as an easier fight against Randy Turpin. The disappointed Sands instead fought on the undercard, beating Mel Brown in the preliminary. Sands won two more fights before returning to Australia. There he awaited a world title match with Robinson, but it was not to be.

Sands's untimely death left his wife and children in dire financial straits. A public appeal was made, and the grief-stricken friends and fans of Dave Sands raised enough money to pay off his home and create a trust fund for his children. He was twenty-six years old.

14. Bobo Olsen. *Courtesy of Gary Youmans.*

Randy Turpin and Bobo Olsen advanced to the title match, as both easily eliminated their opponents, creating an interesting bout between two guys who had both been beaten by Sugar Ray Robinson. Each to his credit had been leading in his fight with the retired champion, with Turpin actually defeating Robinson. Most people thought Olsen had the slight edge. The fight was scheduled for October 21, 1953.

Carl Bobo Olsen was born in Hawaii of Swedish and Portuguese descent. He came by his nickname, Bobo, from his little sister, who would refer to him as her "bobo" instead of her brother. A tough guy, Bobo won on his tenacity and amazing stamina. Olsen was a notoriously slow starter who, if he could get past the first few rounds, would wear people down. In preparation for the Turpin fight he boxed little, sparring fewer than four rounds a day. At twenty-five years old, he was ready for his first real chance at the championship. He was confident that he could beat Randy Turpin.

15. Randy Turpin. *Courtesy of Gary Youmans.*

BOBO OLSEN (Boxer): "This is a dream come true for me. I will win this fight. There is no way over fifteen rounds that Turpin can beat me . . . if it goes that long."

CARMEN BASILIO: "When I was stationed in Hawaii, Bobo was the big star. Every time he fought, everyone would go to his fights but me. I never got to go because I always had guard duty."

On July 10, 1951, Randy Turpin had stunned the boxing world with his upset win over Sugar Ray Robinson in London. Robinson, who was completing his second European tour, prepared badly for Turpin and was soundly beaten. The repeat fight a few months later was closely fought before Sugar Ray knocked Turpin out in the tenth round. The rematch was close for nine rounds, partly due to Turpin's style of boxing. An avid weight lifter, he had become a very physical, rugged fighter who would duck punches by pulling back from the waist. This unorthodox approach confused his opponents. Sugar Ray struggled through both fights in timing his punches. At the beginning of the tenth round the two fighters accidentally butted heads, with Robinson getting the worst of the collision. Blood began to spurt out of a ugly gash over Sugar Ray's left eye. Robinson, sensing that the fight was seconds away from being stopped by referee Rudy Goldstein, attacked Turpin with a vengeance, driving left-right combinations furiously to Turpin's head, finally flooring him with a right to the jaw. Up at the count of nine, Turpin was hit with another barrage of punches, as a blood-soaked Sugar Ray Robinson beat him into submission. Goldstein stepped in, and the fight was over. There were seven seconds left in the round. Afterward, Turpin said he thought Goldstein had stopped the fight too soon, arguing that he was not hurt. The loss angered him, and over a period of time he became less and less friendly toward the British press, which had all but canonized him after his improbable victory over Sugar Ray in London.

Turpin prepared even less than Olsen for this title bout. He was clearly troubled over his devastating loss to Robinson two years before, and the fragility of his psyche started to become more obvious to people. He became easily agitated and constantly argued with his manager, threatening more than once to pack his bags and go home to England. The recently divorced fighter had additional problems with an American woman, Adele Daniels, whom he had met when he was in New York for the second Robinson fight. She badgered him all through his stay and would not leave him alone, which included a couple of public screaming matches. Turpin went into the fight an 11-5 underdog.

●   ●   ●

NEW YORK, OCTOBER 21, 1953. A crowd of 18,869 packed Madison Square Garden to watch a clash between two determined combatants. Turpin, coming in at a light 157 pounds, started fast applying pressure to Olsen from the opening bell. He fired punches from all directions, connecting with two lefts to the side of Olsen's head, which clearly rattled Bobo's cage. Turpin kept up his full-court attack through the first five rounds, but could not put the game Olsen down. Beginning with the sixth round the fight changed, as Olsen began to dominate the fight. Now the aggressor, Bobo attacked Turpin with a series of body shots as the weary Englishman held on. In the seventh, Olsen hooked a left to Turpin's body, followed by a right to the chin that pushed Turpin to the ropes, where Olsen battered him with both hands. After trading punches in the ninth, Olsen forced Turpin into the corner of the ring, where he dropped him with a solid combination to the head. Up at the count of nine, Turpin fought back as the bell sounded. Olsen continued to dominate the fight, with the crowd roaring with every blow delivered. When it was over, both men were treated to a standing ovation.

Turpin and Olsen both seemed relieved that the ordeal for the middleweight crown was over. They had each fought hard throughout the fight, and it was now up to the two judges and referee to decide who was the new champion. Most people in attendance thought Olsen had come back to win the fight. Of course, in boxing, strange things can occur when you add up the cards. When Bobo Olsen heard his name announced as the new middleweight champion of the world, he broke down and wept. He had finally made it to the top of the mountain. He was overcome with emotion. Bobo, after his typically slow beginning, had rallied in the second half of the fight, clearly outboxing Randy Turpin. Each fighter took home $57,492 for his efforts. Turpin, the darling of the British press when he defeated Sugar Ray Robinson in 1951, received much harsher reviews following his loss to Bobo Olsen.

GEORGE WHITING (British Writer): "Randy Turpin's defeat by Bobo Olsen is a ring tragedy that can be explained at the moment only by inadequate training methods."

The *London Evening News* reported it this way: "Sackcloth and ashes and do not look for any excuses. Turpin was well and truly beaten. His 'as I please' training methods clearly didn't work."

On the day prior to his return to England Randy Turpin was accused by Adele Daniels of rape and assault. The case was later settled out of court for thirty-five hundred dollars. His career took a real jolt when a year later he was knocked out in Rome, Italy, in the first round by light-hitting Tiberio Mitri. Later, he won the British and Empire light heavyweight titles, with his career coming to a close in 1958, when he was knocked out by Yolande Pompey.

Randy Turpin retired broke. All the money he had made fighting was gone. The Inland Revenue began hounding him for back taxes on his boxing winnings that he had never bothered to file. In May 1966, feeling unwanted and deep in debt, Randy Turpin purchased a gun and with his four-year-old daughter, Carmen, in hand went up to his attic bedroom. He first shot his young daughter, then put the gun to his head and pulled the trigger. A few hours later his wife found his slumped body on the floor. He was dead. Luckily, Carmen had survived the shooting. Randy Turpin was thirty-seven years old.

Bobo Olsen flew home to San Francisco early the following morning, anxious to share the biggest moment of his career with his wife, Dolores, and their four children. When city officials offered to have a parade to celebrate his great victory, Olsen said no. Despite Olsen's protests, more than three hundred friends and well-wishers greeted his plane when it touched down.

BOBO OLSEN (Boxer): "I was confident going into the fight. I didn't get much of a chance in the first three rounds, but I seemed to be better by the fourth. I landed a couple of good punches to the body and when I saw Randy blinking his eyes I knew I had just stunned him. After that I just waded in."

After winning the middleweight championship, Bobo Olsen humbly paid homage to his friend Dave Sands: "If Dave Sands were still alive . . . he would be wearing this belt."

16. New York City Police Department mug shot of
Frankie Carbo.

6.

The Gray

james D. Norris, the new power broker in boxing, had the business connections to get things done. He could pick up the telephone and at a moment's notice talk with practically any chief executive officer in the United States. If he didn't know them personally, then he knew someone who did. His sphere of influence was enormous. He appreciated his position in life yet chose to keep people at a distance. He had the social skills and charm to make friends easily but never allowed anyone to get too close to him. He liked the limelight, being out front leading the parade, but always went home alone to a mysterious private life. Few people were let in.

Over the years he came to enjoy the company of gangsters and gamblers. He was intrigued by their lifestyle and they with him. Mob guys liked being seen in the company of a wealthy, refined man such as James D. Norris. They had their needs, and he had his. Soon after his and Wirtz's International Boxing Clubs were formed, Norris recognized that despite the control and power they now wielded, they needed some muscle on the back end to protect their interests. They needed someone who could ensure that boxers and their managers worked exclusively with them and their associated arenas. He knew the mentality of the people involved in boxing and the cutthroats that prospered within it. People with Harvard business degrees need not apply. A degree from the streets was required for this job. He quickly identified the right guy for the job, the biggest mobster involved in the fight game, Frankie Carbo.

Paul John Carbo, known as Frankie Carbo, was born on August 10, 1904, in New York City. His criminal record went back to 1915, when at the age of eleven he was sent to the Catholic Protectory. A lifetime of crime included seventeen arrests for vagrancy, suspicious character, felonious assault, grand larceny, robbery, and murder. His first murder charge, in 1924, was for killing a taxi driver. After being on the lam for four years, he copped a plea of manslaughter and was sentenced to two to four years in Sing Sing. He served two years of his sentence.

He was arrested again in 1931, 1936, and 1939, all on charges of suspected murder. The last killing involved gunning down a member of Murder Incorporated, Harry "Big Greenie" Greenburg. In court, Al Tannenbaum, another member of Murder Inc., testified that Carbo and Bugsy Siegel killed Greenburg as he was coming out of his house. According to Tannebaum, Carbo was the killer, putting five slugs in Big Greenie, while Siegel drove the getaway car. The trial ended with a hung jury when the key witness, strangely, fell out of a hotel window. Carbo and Siegel were never retried for the homicide.

In public, Frankie Carbo was always dressed impeccably, with an engaging demeanor to match. Nicknamed "the Gray" because of his penchant for wearing gray suits, Carbo was a man who wielded immense power. He would hold court at the Forrest Hotel in New York City, surrounded by a gang of yes men, commonly referred to as his "beards." On the surface he appeared to be an easy mark for somebody down on their luck, but he was not a man to be crossed. Regardless of what he did for anyone down the line he was always going to get paid. He could magically move average fighters along to where they became contenders, sometimes winning championships. Of course, there were strings attached when "doing business" with Carbo. Fighters had to agree to take a "dive" from time to time on Carbo's request. His wrath knew no boundaries, and the terror he could inflict on people that dared cross him was imposing.

TEDDY BRENNER (coauthor of *Only the Ring Was Square*): "In 1951, Billy Graham was signed to fight Kid Gavilan for the world welterweight championship in Madison Square Garden. A few days before the fight, Irving Cohen got word that Frankie Carbo wanted to see him. When Carbo called . . . people answered. He was described by the newspapers as the 'underworld's overlord of boxing.' Irving went to see Carbo at the bar in the old Forrest Hotel on 49th Street, down the block from the Garden.

"'You want your boy should be champ?' Carbo says.

"'Sure of course,' Irving said. 'That's what he is fighting Gavilan for.'

"'You give me twenty percent of him and you get the title,' Carbo says.

"'Frank I can't give you twenty percent,' the manager said. 'I got a piece and there's Jack Reilly . . . who brought Billy to me. He's got a piece. There ain't room for you.'

"'Talk to the fighter. He's the one that's got the say.'

"So Irving talked to Graham, and he didn't go for it. When Cohen told Carbo there was no deal, Carbo said, "'Does this kid know he ain't going to win?'

"'He knows,' Irving said.

"'He's got a lot to learn about life,' Carbo said."

Kid Gavilan later won by a decision that night in Madison Square Garden even though Billy Graham had clearly won the fight.

Frankie Carbo's top lieutenant in boxing was Frank "Blinky" Palermo, a Philadelphia numbers runner who in the 1940s and early 1950s was a licensed boxing manager. Palermo, just over five feet tall with a large, protruding nose, was an arrogant little man. He had a police record that included larceny and assault. Palermo managed a number of fighters, including Billy Fox, Johnny Saxton, and Ike Williams. Williams had won the NBA lightweight championship in 1945 before becoming world lightweight champion in 1947. He held the title until 1951, when he was knocked out by Jimmy Carter in New York. A tough fighter with above-average punching power, Williams went to Palermo for help after he was blackballed by the Managers' Guild following a dispute with his then manager, Connie McCarthy. Unable to secure fights, he turned to Palermo, who quickly smoothed things over with the guild. His career then took off. He insists he never took any dives for Palermo but did admit to carrying some fighters from time to time.

IKE WILLIAMS: "I turned down an offer by Blinky Palermo of thirty thousand dollars to throw a fight that I eventually lost. I should have taken the money."

It was a powerful alliance that James D. Norris formed with "the Gray." The tentacles of this grouping of the rich man and the thug would reach deep into boxing's soft underbelly, affecting the way some fighters fought, some writers wrote, and champions were crowned. It was there for the taking, and they took.

ADA ROTHSCHILD (Wife): "My husband, Norm, and I were in Montreal for a fight, and Frankie Carbo was there, and they announced him from the ring as the 'honorable Frankie Carbo.' Norm and I couldn't believe it. He stood up and took a bow."

17. A typical boxing gym in the 1950s. *Courtesy of Carmen Basilio.*

7.

Locker Room Stories

the *strongest muscle in the body is the tongue.*

CARMEN BASILIO: "My father was an avid hunter and a great shot. When we went hunting with him and we shot and missed, he would get mad at us. When you aimed, you had better hit your target, or you were going to hear about it."

ROCKY MARCIANO: "A guy who's got a chance to be champion, is a dope to let it go. You can get rich. You can make friends, you can be something even if you're nobody starting out like me."

CARMEN BASILIO: "A fighter starts off with nothing, and he knows that by winning more fights he's going to get up to the top . . . he'll have more . . . he'll fight harder, and naturally he's more hungry, so he's going to fight harder. That's what makes a hungry fighter, and that's what makes 'em get to the top."

ANGELO DUNDEE (Basilio Cornerman): "Before a fight I try to keep my fighters loose as a goose. I always have a joke or two for them. I tell them to let it 'all hang out,' that this is their time. Once the fight starts I say little. Too much bullshit can ruin a fighter. I'm a 'We Guy' instead of being an 'I Guy.' I try to visualize during a fight what I would do if I was in there and pass it on to the fighter. I pay attention to the store."

A writer once asked boxer Tony Pellone what he did with his money. "Whatever money I make I take home to my old man, and he would give me five dollars out of it," Pellone answered. "Then the time I fought Bob Montgomery at the Garden I got $8,513 for

18. Carmen with his hunting dogs. *Courtesy of Carmen Basilio.*

my end. So I took it home and I gave it to my old man and he said to me in Italian, 'How you fixed?' I said that I'm broke. 'All right,' he said. 'Here.' He gave me thirteen dollars. I said, 'Hey, thirteen is unlucky. Give me fourteen dollars instead.' Then my old man said, 'No, give me one dollar back. That makes twelve.'"

WILLIE PASTRANO (Boxer, when asked by the ring doctor if he knew where he was): "You're damn right I do. I'm in Madison Square Garden getting the crap knocked out of me."

CARMEN BASILIO: "I pray before every fight that the fight is a good fight and that both of us come out uninjured and I always ask for extra powers to win. It's my belief that if you ask God for help he will give it to you. That is the way I believe in God."

ADA ROTHSCHILD (Wife): "Johnny DeJohn was a good guy. I thought he was great. Norm and him worked well together. They

19. The Basilio family and friends gather around the dinner table.
Courtesy of Carmen Basilio.

always were fair with each other. When Norm was trying to make a fight between Joey DeJohn and [Robert] Villemain, his handlers said Villemain had to have a guarantee or he wouldn't fight. When Norm heard this he got up to leave, saying there would be no guarantee. Johnny pulled him aside and told him if it doesn't make the money, we will help you with our end."

GREG SORRENTINO (Boxer): "Many Italian American generations from the past had nothing. Even though they had nothing they were still sitting at the dinner table having a good time with always enough to eat. That was the Basilio family. Carmen loved his folks so much."

ANGELO DUNDEE (Basilio Cornerman): "My brother Chris originally hooked me up with Carmen. He needed a cornerman for his fight against Baby Williams, and I got the job. The first time

I met him he scared the hell out of me. He said, 'I just want you to know I cut easily.' That's the last thing a cutman wants to hear. Well, he was right. He'd start bleeding at the weigh-in."

WILLIE PEP (Boxer, talking to an old opponent years after each retired): "'Do you recognize me?' the old opponent asked. Willie looked hard and considered before finally replying, 'Lie down so I can recognize you.'"

ANGELO DUNDEE (Basilio Cornerman): "To be a good boxer you have to have a type of mentality that is rare. You could say boxers are rare people, and Carmen Basilio is the rarest of boxers. There has never been anyone quite like him. A stand-up guy who would out-work anybody to achieve his goal. He's number one in my book."

GREG SORRENTINO (Boxer): "The thing with boxing is you have to live a different life. It is your ass every time you go out there. It's not 'We'll get 'em next week.' You realize that one punch—from somebody who knows how to throw a punch—could kill you. You have to be in the best condition, and your reflexes have to be at their best."

Ray Robinson's nickname, "Sugar Ray," came from sportswriter Jack Case. After watching young Ray show off his wonderful boxing skills, Case commented, "He was sure a sweet fighter." George Gainford replied, "Yeah, sweet as sugar, he's Sugar Ray Robinson." Later Case began to refer to Robinson by this new nickname in his boxing columns.

WILLIE PEP (Boxer): "I've got it made. I've got a wife and a TV set, and they're both working."

JIMMY CANNON (Writer): "Once I was standing at the lunch counter drinking coffee with Eddie Walker, the fight manager. He turned and there was Chalky Wright, then the featherweight champion of the world. The fighter needed a shave, and his stubble of a beard was white. 'Go down and get a shave,' Walker told him. 'I told you not to come around here without a shave. They'll pick up your license you look so old. You could be your own father.'"

MAX BAER (Boxer): "Fear is standing across the ring from Joe Louis and knowing he wants to go home early."

JACK BLACKBURN (Joe Louis Trainer): "Fighting is a tough business. You just gotta throw your heart away when you pull on those gloves, or the other fella will knock it out of you."

FLOYD PATTERSON (Boxer): "A good punch is something that you're born with. Anybody can throw a hard blow if he lets go with all his might, but the trick is in the timing, to beat the other fellow to it. I set my eyes on his chest. That way I can tell every move my opponent is about to make. There's no sense looking at his fists, because that's the last thing he moves. You have to anticipate his punch. By watching his chest I can see it before it starts."

CHARLEY GOLDMAN (Rocky Marciano's Trainer): "The punch you throw will take care of itself. It's the next one you gotta have ready; and if you're ever been knocked down, don't be no hero and jump right up. Take a count."

CARMEN BASILIO: "I know I need plenty of advice, but when you are out there fighting it's the loneliest place in the whole world, and you're concentrating so hard, you don't hear a thing."

20. International Boxing Club hierarchy coming out of federal court. *Courtesy of Carmen Basilio.*

8.

1954

in late summer 1951, a black man by the name of Oliver Brown tried to register his daughter in an all-white school in Topeka, Kansas. Brown's daughter Linda was being forced to travel twenty-one blocks by bus to attend an all-black school when there was a white school just seven blocks from their home. After listening to Brown's request, the Topeka School Board rudely turned him down. Angered over his treatment, the mild-mannered Brown decided to sue the school district over its decision. His case worked its way through the judicial system, finally reaching the doorstep of the Supreme Court in 1954. After considerable review and discussion, the court ruled in favor of Brown, formally ending legal segregation. Now getting people to comply with the highest court in the land's decision was a totally different matter, but black people were now granted greater rights and freedoms. Segregationists could no longer take the moral position that their behavior was based on the law. This landmark decision spurred a civil rights movement, led by Dr. Martin Luther King Jr. America would see a firestorm of protest on both sides of this issue for the remainder of the decade.

EARL WARREN (U.S. Supreme Court Chief Justice): "We conclude that in the court of public opinion the doctrine of 'separate but equal' has no place. Separate educational facilities are inherently unequal."

The sport of professional boxing was also in serious legal review in 1954, centering on its manner of doing business. On February 15, 1954, U.S. District Court judge Gregory F. Noonan determined that boxing was not a business or a monopoly; it was, in his opinion, a sport similar to baseball. Using the Supreme Court's position on baseball as a precedent, the judge threw out the federal monopoly case against boxing. Judge Noonan believed that the Supreme Court's recent decision, in 1953, placed all sports outside the Sherman Anti-Trust Act. The Sherman Act, authored by Senator John Sherman of Ohio, was signed into law by President Benjamin Harrison in 1890.

THE SHERMAN ACT: "Every person who shall monopolize or attempt to monopolize or combine or conspire with any other person or persons, to monopolize any part of the trade or commerce among several states or with foreign nations, shall be deemed guilty of a felony."

The federal government appealed Judge Noonan's decision in 1954, arguing that the manner in which boxing was presently doing business violated the country's laws against monopolies. The government's position was that it should be allowed to pursue an antitrust suit against boxing. The intention of the government suit was not so much to affect the industry of boxing but to restore fair and equal competition. The argument boiled down to whether the widespread use of television contracts by boxing promoters placed them in interstate commerce. The government said yes . . . boxing said no.

The defendants named in the suit were the New York and Illinois International Boxing Clubs, the Madison Square Garden Corporation, James Norris, and Arthur Wirtz. It was pointed out that the defendants had promoted nineteen of twenty-one championship fights in the United States between June 1949 and April 1954. The root of the problem was Norris and Wirtz's two International Boxing Clubs: They were making large sums of money promoting boxing. They made this money because they controlled boxing in a very monopolistic manner. They had exclusive contracts to promote fights in all the main arenas across the country, including Madison Square Garden. They had the boxers locked into personal service contracts, and they had the lucrative television contracts.

The government's position was that if it looks like a duck, walks like a duck, and quacks like a duck, then it's a monopoly. Norris and Wirtz were beginning to feel the heat regarding the manner in which they were conducting business.

Carmen Basilio, on the strength of his performance against Kid Gavilan in 1953, should have been given another crack at the popular Cuban champion. Unfortunately for Basilio, James Norris and Frankie Carbo had other "plans" regarding the welterweight crown. First, Carbo decided to give Johnny Bratton another chance at the title, followed by a title match with Johnny Saxton, the fighter of his top lieutenant, Blinky Palermo.

Herman "Hymie" Wallman was a friend of Carbo, and he had become Johnny Bratton's manager through Carbo's influence with James Norris. Wallman, a manufacturer of mink coats, loved boxing and had expressed an interest in becoming Bratton's manager after watching him fight in 1950. A meeting was arranged for Wallman with James Norris in Chicago, with Truman Gibson and Carbo also present. The price agreed upon was $12,500. Wallman took the deal with one caveat: he would not have to put any money down; the money owed to Norris would be deducted from Bratton's purses. Norris at first rejected the counteroffer by Wallman, but was later convinced by Carbo to accept Wallman's proposal.

HERMAN WALLMAN: "Frankie Carbo played the part that he recommended me to the IBC people. He told them that I was an honest guy and that they would not lose money with me."

Kid Gavilan easily outboxed Johnny Bratton over fifteen rounds in Chicago to retain his title, setting up his match with Johnny Saxton. Gavilan, unfortunately, had to postpone his match with Saxton twice because of an injured right hand and then a case of mumps. The veteran boxer was beginning to show some wear and tear from all the fighting he had done over his lifetime. He now struggled to make the welterweight limit of 147 pounds. Despite all his problems, he entered the fight a 2-1 favorite.

The Pennsylvania Athletic Commission chairman, Frank Weiner, concerned about Gavilan making the weight, ruled that no

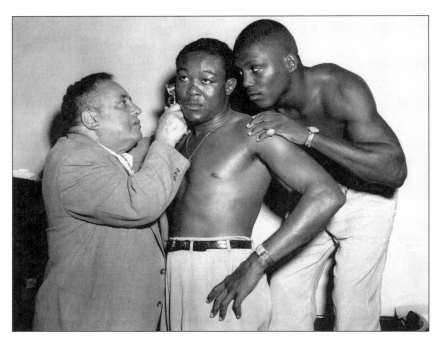

21. Kid Gavilan and Johnny Saxton getting their prefight physicals. *Courtesy of AP Images.*

matter what happened when Gavilan stepped on the scales, his state would be hosting a championship bout. It may not be for the world welterweight title, but it would be for what Weiner referred to as "the prestigious Pennsylvania welterweight crown." Fortunately for the seventy-nine hundred who showed up at the Philadelphia Convention Hall and a national television audience, Gavilan made the 147-pound limit.

Johnny Saxton was a good boxer who, despite backroom maneuvering, had earned a title shot, coming into the fight with a 43-2-2 record. An orphan, raised in Harlem, Saxton was extremely hyperactive, and his mental stability was in question. Recently convicted of twelve traffic violations in New York, he was scheduled to begin serving a fifteen-day jail sentence the day after the fight. The young fighter had learned to box at the orphanage, carving out a very solid amateur career, winning thirty-one out of thirty-three fights. He won the Golden Gloves as a lightweight in 1948. His only two losses as a professional were to solid fighters, Gil Turner and Del Flanigan. Included in his forty-three victories were impressive wins over Joey Giardello and Ralph "Tiger" Jones. Kid Gavilan predicted that Saxton would give him a good fight for five rounds—after that, he would take him apart like he did Johnny Bratton. The fight would not be close.

•   •   •

PHILADELPHIA, OCTOBER 19, 1954. Johnny Saxton, in one of the strangest unanimous decisions in boxing history, stole the welterweight crown from an aging Kid Gavilan. Both ring judges and referee Pete Pantalo voted for Saxton as the clear victor, even though nineteen out of twenty-one writers polled following the fight had Gavilan the winner. The match, clearly one of the poorest fought in many years, was boring from the opening bell. Prior to the sixth round, an exasperated commission chairman, Weiner, told referee Pantalo to instruct the boxers "to do some fighting." Neither boxer initiated any attack, content to waltz around the ring. The disappointed Convention Hall fans so supportive of the underdog Saxton at the start of the fight now rained "boos" on the two noncombatants. Saxton, a very competent boxer, spent a great deal of the time grabbing and holding on to Gavilan. At the beginning of the seventh round Saxton screamed at Gavilan, *"Come out and fight!"* When the champion sought to attack Saxton inside, he found himself again being tightly held. Near the end of the fight, no longer fearing the light-hitting Gavilan, the challenger began to box. Saxton's efforts recharged his fans, but he did little damage to the champion. Following the fight Chairman Weiner attempted to put a positive slant on a very suspect result, saying that he thought Saxton was the "busier fighter of the two" and deserved to win. Weiner added that overall he was not pleased with the way the two fighters had conducted themselves throughout the majority of the fifteen-round fight.

KID GAVILAN: "This fight was very bad, but it not my fault. If you have man in ring who does not want to fight there is nothing you can do about it. I talk to Saxton in clinches and beg him to start fighting. When that didn't work, I complain to referee but he do nothing. I don't like to talk about fixed fights because I don't know anything about them but I can't help wondering what those judges were thinking as Saxton held me locked in his arms. They must give him one point credit for every second he held me. I don't want nothing that I don't deserve, but I win at least nine rounds."

DAN PARKER (Writer): "Jack Kerns told some friends before the fight to send in all they had on Saxton who, he said, couldn't lose. In New York many fans who tried to put money on Saxton were told that they could bet only on Gavilan. After the fight, [Blinky] Palermo said there would be no return match for Gavilan. And before and after it, Goombar Carbo lavishly entertained fight mobsters from all over America at a hotel suite. He had good reason to celebrate."

FAUSTO MIRANDA (Writer): "The gangsters robbed Gavilan. Let us say that all of Latin America is now going through this moment of witnessing the down fall of a great idol and a great champion by the bad faith of some judges. Gavilan was defeated by the behind-the-door maneuvers of racketeers, the real owners of the pugilistic business in North America."

Kid Gavilan, a few days following his loss to Johnny Saxton, attended a party thrown by Frankie Carbo. He walked up to Carbo and asked, "Mr. Carbo, Blinky Palermo told me that they do whatever you want. That's what he told me. And if that what you told . . . for what they do to me . . . I would like a rematch."

"Right," Carbo said.

The next day, the lawyer of newly crowned welterweight champion Johnny Saxton made an eloquent plea for leniency for his client, stating that he was a quiet, self-effacing, reticent individual who understood the severity of his actions. Saxton's lawyer went on to suggest that any further punishment would be no worse than what he has already suffered. He hinted that "this black cloud" that had been following his client contributed to his lackluster performance the night before, which almost cost him the welterweight championship. Similar to the night before in Pennsylvania, Saxton received another gift from a judge.

JOHN M. MURTAUGH (Chief Justice of New York): "Mr. Saxton you are not entitled to any consideration but because of the eloquent plea of your attorney on your behalf, I am going to suspend execution of the sentence, but I warn you don't let it happen again."

JOHNNY SAXTON: "Thank you your honor. You will never see me in a courtroom again. I have learned my lesson."

The next day Mundito Medina, Kid Gavilan's trainer, indicated that Gavilan had an "ironclad" contract for a rematch within ninety days. The International Boxing Clubs, which had copromoted the Wednesday-night bout, quickly released a statement through managing director Harry Markson that there was no signed contract in place for a return match. No further negotiations were conducted.

Four days following Saxton's win over Kid Gavilan, the New York State Athletic Commission ruled that Saxton's first defense of his title should be against Carmen Basilio. Any other engagement by the new champion would not be recognized by the state. "We will not sanction any title match between Saxton and anybody but Basilio," New York chairman Robert K. Christenberry strongly stated. Christenberry indicated that he was going to ask the World Boxing Championship Committee, when it met in London the following month, to support the New York edict. Christenberry went on to say that he would also solicit the commission to support a rule that would make it mandatory for titleholders to meet top-rated contenders designated by the committee. Saxton had been rated anywhere from first to third by experts. Basilio was generally considered the top-ranked welterweight contender in the world.

Frankie Carbo and James Norris were not considering giving Basilio a shot at the title just yet. There was one more marker that needed to be taken care of before Basilio got to center stage. It involved Carbo's old friend from Boston, Anthony "Rip" Valenti. His kid would get first crack at the suspect champion.

Kid Gavilan never fought for a world title again. He hung around boxing until 1958, fighting all over the world but never again with the zest that had made him a crowd favorite. His 10-15-1 record belies the sadness of his fall from grace. He later lost his sight.

22. Program cover featuring Tony DeMarco and
Carmen Basilio, 1955. *Courtesy of Don Hamilton.*

9.

"Mr. Blood and Guts" Meets "Mr. Blood and Guts"

tony DeMarco was born Leonard Liotta on January 14, 1932. Tony, one of four children, grew up in the tough North End section of Boston. He took the name Tony DeMarco when he was fifteen years old so he would be eligible to fight in the Boston Amateur Program.

TONY DEMARCO: "I was only fifteen. You had to be sixteen to get into the amateurs. A friend of mine named Tony DeMarco was sixteen so I took his name and his birth certificate. Later on he wanted to box but he can't be Tony DeMarco, because that's me, so he takes the name of another kid on the block, Michael Temini. Later, he wants to box and he takes the name of some other kid."

DeMarco was a southpaw, and his idea of boxing when he began was to just keep punching until someone told him to stop or the bell rang. His tremendous desire caught the attention of Mike Nazzaro, who worked in the neighboring parks department. Nazzaro convinced him to join their youth boxing program, which eventually paved the way for him to get into tournaments. He won twelve out of fourteen fights during his amateur career, losing once to future professional boxer George Araujo and another time because of a cut eye. The family short on money, Tony DeMarco turned pro in 1948. DeMarco won his first seven matches, six by knockout, before suffering his first loss, to Edward White in October 1949. Over the next three years, Tony won twenty-four of his twenty-five matches, fourteen by knockout. Like so many boxers of that era, Tony DeMarco lacked the proper management, and his career appeared to be headed nowhere. Frustrated, he decided to try his luck north of the border in 1952.

TONY DEMARCO: "I was winning but that didn't mean much. I had to get a 'name' for myself, but it looked like a long tough grind and I got disgusted. I couldn't see any profit just barely covering my living expenses, so I lit out for Montreal to try my luck. It was worse. I not only was getting no money but I was getting licked. That was rubbing it in too much. After I lost to Brian Kelley and Gene Poirer I got so disgusted I decided to chuck this whole fight business."

DeMarco stayed away from boxing for more than a year before he made the acquaintance of Anthony "Rip" Valenti. Valenti put DeMarco in touch with two experienced boxing men, Sammy Fuller and Frankie Campbell. DeMarco's career took off as Fuller began sharpening Tony's fighting skills while helping him define his ring style.

TONY DEMARCO: "I wasn't a very good boxer when I started. Rip got me working with Sammy Fuller in the gym. He had fought guys like Jimmy McLarin and Barney Ross in his career, so he knew what he was talking about. He had been there. He taught me a lot."

The young boxer won fifteen fights in a row, now drawing comparisons to heavyweight champion Rocky Marciano in his warrior approach to fighting. He was Rocky, just in a smaller body. By January 1955, *Ring Magazine* had him rated as the sixth-best welterweight in the world. After DeMarco fought lightweight champion Jimmy Carter to a draw, the well-connected Valenti got him a shot at the welterweight title. The bout was scheduled for Boston on April Fools' Day, 1955.

●   ●   ●

BOSTON, APRIL 1, 1955. The misunderstood Johnny Saxton, the fighter many boxing fans and writers believed had stolen the welterweight crown from Kid Gavilan, came to fight that night. He entered the ring determined to put to rest the notion that he was a "paper champion." He had much to prove. Both fighters, from the opening bell, exacted a huge amount of physical pain on each other with aggressive fighting. The "DeMarco Plan" was to attack the champion's midsection, which would eventually wear him down. Saxton's plan was to fight hard each round and disprove the notion that he wasn't a worthy champion. Little by little the DeMarco Plan won out, as the challenger's vicious body blows began to take a toll on Saxton. Finally, in the fourteenth round, the Boston Bull Dog caught up with his quarry, connecting on two solid left hooks to Saxton's jaw and dropping him to the canvas. The champion, sprawled out with part of his body outside the ropes, struggled to get up as referee Mel Manning's count reached five. Somehow, Saxton got to his feet, but DeMarco, with his fists blazing, went after him, pummeling him with punch after punch. DeMarco pinned the now defenseless Saxton against the rope before Manning stepped in and stopped the fight. The kid from the North End was now king of the welterweights. Tony DeMarco had done it the old-fashioned way, standing toe-to-toe and slugging it out with his opponent. This five-foot-five-inch dynamo was the first Boston champion since Honey Mellody had won the welterweight crown back in 1906. The Boston Garden fans were so excited about DeMarco's improbable win that they crowded around the ring to get a closer look at Boston's new "golden boy."

In his dressing room, Johnny Saxton was crestfallen over his loss to Tony DeMarco, a fighter he had been favored to beat. Neither he nor his manager, Blinky Palermo, had seen this result coming, or they never would have accepted the fight. The press had to wait for more than an hour before Saxton and his manager would agree to speak with them. Saxton in defeat had in some ways earned a measure of victory, showing tremendous heart and purpose throughout the fight. To many fight fans, Saxton had looked more like a champion losing to Tony DeMarco than he had beating Kid Gavilan. He was confident his manager had the connections to get a rematch within ninety days, and he would get his crown back. Little did he know that night, his head throbbing in pain, his lip bleeding, and his heart broken, that he would have to wait. There would be no ninety-day rematch. Frankie Carbo and Jim Norris didn't care about him or what was in his best interest. They already knew whom DeMarco would take on next. It had to do with the "onion picker" from Canastota. He had been put on the shelf for too long. The fighter who the public was demanding get another title shot was on deck.

John DeJohn and Joe Nitro attended the DeMarco-Saxton fight in Boston compliments of the International Boxing Club. Sitting ringside, they were both impressed by the way DeMarco took Saxton out in the fourteenth round. He had fought with the same determination that Basilio fought with, displaying a fearlessness in his approach, willing to take two punches to be able to deliver one. Basilio, DeJohn observed, was slightly bigger than DeMarco, and the Syracuse trainer thought his guy was the better puncher. Also, Joe Nitro pointed out that nobody really gave DeMarco much of a chance against Saxton, which definitely worked to his advantage. They both knew there would be no overconfidence on Basilio's part if these two met in the ring. No question, it would be a real "donnybrook."

On returning to Syracuse, DeJohn received a call from Gabe Genovese about a proposed match between Basilio and DeMarco. Genovese, a barber by trade, was the nephew of Vito Genovese. In the 1930s, he had comanaged with Frankie Carbo middleweight champion Babe Risko. He and Carbo over the years had become very close friends. Genovese told DeJohn that he would be happy to speak with Carbo about finalizing the plans for Basilio to get another title shot. Genovese said that he could put this fight together, but it was going to come at a price—it would cost Basilio five thousand dollars. DeJohn, anxious to get his guy a shot at De-Marco, agreed to the money. He wanted no delays or problems with this fight coming off. He told Genovese that first they would have to get Basilio's okay on it, but he would see that it all worked out. DeJohn would get back in touch with Genovese after he had talked to Carmen. The cost of doing business was going up, but what options did DeJohn have? He either worked with these people, or they would freeze Basilio out.

John DeJohn and Joe Nitro went to Basilio's house that night to explain the situation. DeJohn told Carmen that Genovese's relationship with Carbo would ensure the fight would be arranged through the IBC. There would be no strings attached other than it was going to cost them five thousand dollars. Basilio sat silently, staring straight ahead. Finally, he turned toward DeJohn, stood up, and looked DeJohn straight in the eyes. "John, I'm not going to give those bastards a dime. They don't deserve crap. They can't deny me forever—the public won't stand for it. Don't you understand that? Eventually, I'm going to get my chance."

"Carmen, If we don't give them a piece of the purse, there will be no fight."

"Baloney. If they get paid, it comes out of you and Joe's side . . . But I don't want to know anything about it. The hell with those guys. I'll punch them in the mouth if they come near me. John, it's not right what they are trying to do."

John DeJohn knew it was pointless to argue with Basilio about doing business with the Mob. Carmen despised them, and that wasn't going to change. There was no sense in getting him any angrier. He would have to handle this by himself. DeJohn and Joe Nitro drove home in silence, both knowing a tough decision needed to be made. The next morning DeJohn called Genovese and told him to make the fight.

● ● ●

Averell Harriman took office in January 1955 as the new governor of New York State, replacing Thomas E. Dewey. In defeating Dewey, Harriman became the first Democrat to hold that office in twelve years. One of Governor Harriman's first orders of business was to hire a new chairman of the New York State

Athletic Commission, replacing the ineffective Robert Christenberry. A fifty-two-year-old former district attorney from Brooklyn, Julius Helfand, was chosen. Helfand, a tough, hard-nosed prosecutor, had developed a reputation as the foremost expert on crime in the United States. The change, on the surface, appeared political because Helfand was a Democrat, but Helfand would approach his new position with a zeal and understanding of the type of people he would be dealing with that Robert Christenberry never did.

JULIUS HELFAND: "I accepted the appointment because it gives me an opportunity to do real public service. I believe I can do a good job. If I didn't think so I would not have quit the job I had. I want to explore the workings of the Commission before taking any action. I have heard there may be a number of things wrong with the boxing situation. I intend to investigate to find out."

Helfand took a $1,500 pay cut to become the new chairman, with a salary of $13,500 annually. A man known to be very thorough in his investigations, he had many issues to deal with upon taking office, most of which were about restoring the confidence of the people in the sport of boxing. It would be a tall order. The infiltration of the Mob into boxing, fights being fixed, and organizations such as the International Boxing Club of New York running roughshod over the commission were all on Helfand's plate when he assumed the role as chairman. The man he replaced, Bob Christenberry, had been beaten down by the Mob and the IBC, but this time around they would be dealing with a completely different breed of cat.

In early May 1955, Helfand began conducting inquiries into alleged irregularities in the conduct of boxing in New York State. The new chairman of the New York State Athletic Commission was investigating supposed sanctions against boxer Vince Martinez, who had been blackballed by fight managers through their organization, the International Boxing Guild. Martinez, a year earlier, had gotten into an argument over money with his manager, William Daly, who happened to be an officer in the Managers'

Guild. In support of Daly, the guild had gotten the word out to all its members not to schedule any fights with Martinez. He appealed to the New York State Athletic Commission for help. After much testimony, it became clear that Martinez was being unfairly boycotted.

During the course of the commission's hearings, it uncovered an unbelievable amount of arrogance on the part of the managers, who believed they had every right to prevent Martinez from fighting. Also, it was revealed in testimony that each guild member was required to pay a $100 fee each time one of his fighters fought in a main event anywhere in the United States. This "tribute" was also to be paid by all nonmembers in the form of advertising fees. It was reported that Ray Arcel had forked over $17,000 toward the guild's monthly periodical, the *International Boxing Magazine*. Arcel understood that if he didn't pay these "advertising fees," he would not have any guild-managed boxers for his Saturday-night telecasts, essentially putting him out of business. The guild handled all the top boxers across the country, and its members were unified in their position regarding the $100 fee.

The commission also discovered during the three weeks of testimony that the International Boxing Club supported the guild's position. After questioning the IBC's managing director, Harry Markson, Helfand called for its president to appear before the commission. Helfand wanted James Norris to shed some more light on the Martinez situation and other issues regarding IBC practices. On May 20, 1955, Jim Norris appeared at the New York State Athletic Commission offices on West Forty-seventh Street in New York City, just a short distance from Broadway. Truman Gibson accompanied Norris as his legal counsel. Julius Helfand began his interrogation by asking the president of the IBC of New York if he had discussed with anyone the boycott of Vince Martinez. Norris, sitting erect in his chair, told Helfand that he was not totally familiar with the Martinez case, but he assured the new chairman that he had never spoken with anyone regarding a Martinez boycott. Finally, after about fifteen minutes of questioning, Helfand moved closer to Norris, smiling at the IBC president, and began a different line of questioning.

HELFAND: "Do you know a man named Frankie Carbo?"

NORRIS: "Yes."

HELFAND: "How long have you known him?"

NORRIS: "Twenty years."

HELFAND: "Have you ever discussed the promotion of any fights with Mr. Carbo?"

NORRIS: "No, I haven't."

HELFAND: "What is Mr. Carbo's business to your knowledge?"

NORRIS: "I couldn't answer that."

HELFAND: "You don't know?"

NORRIS: "No."

HELFAND: "In twenty years you haven't been able to find out what his business is?"

NORRIS: "I am not a social friend of Mr. Carbo's, Mr. Chairman. I know Mr. Carbo. I talk to him. I have a cup of coffee with him occasionally."

HELFAND: "Would you say that is a normal and natural thing during an association of friendship of twenty years to find out a man's business, what he really does for a living?"

NORRIS: "I think you misconstrued something. You asked me how long I had known Frankie Carbo . . . not how long I had been friends with him."

HELFAND: "You said you knew him twenty years?"

NORRIS: "Yes, I would say that I have seen him around and have said hello to him for twenty years."

HELFAND: "Other than fights, where have you seen Mr. Carbo?"

NORRIS: "I don't recall seeing him at fights, Mr. Chairman. I have seen him occasionally at the race track, possibly at a restaurant around town, something like that."

HELFAND: "Have you ever heard it said that Mr. Carbo had a financial interest, or a piece of fighters?"

NORRIS: "I have read that for twenty years."

HELFAND: "Have you ever heard it in the trade other than having read it?"

NORRIS: "No."

HELFAND: "Have you ever discussed with Mr. Carbo fights or fighters?"

NORRIS: "No."

James Norris was excused.

The commission had heard fifteen hundred pages of testimony regarding the Managers' Guild of New York, which was publicly revealed to be an arm of the two International Boxing Clubs. Helfand would now take the information gathered and carefully decide the proper course of action. It would take five months before a decision was released.

James Norris, feeling the pressure being now applied by the government and the New York State Athletic Commission, went on the offensive, telling writer Dan Daniel of *Ring Magazine* in the September 1955 issue, *"I won't let them kill Boxing."*

JAMES D. NORRIS: "I am not going to let them kill boxing. This is a great sport. That is not a discovery of my own. It is a sport that has been under sharp criticism from the very year of its inception in England, and never has been free of the carping blast in this country. Yet, here it is, very much alive and thriving. What keeps it alive? The criticism? No. The inherent strength of the sport. Let me make this very emphatic. I would like it to be the one point I put across in this interview, if I put over no other. If boxing were as wrong as so many newspapers and magazines have made it out to be, I would not be in it. Nor would my associates be in it. Please make that as definite as you possibly can. I don't make a living out of boxing. I don't have to remain in the sport for my coffee and toast. I am in boxing because I love it and because it's worth my efforts. I am running the International Boxing Club . . . I and I alone and no undercover operator, Carbo or anybody else. I am not forced to be more than civil to anybody in the USA. I don't have to kowtow to anybody. I don't kowtow to Carbo or anybody connected with Carbo. I have been accused of bringing persons into the fight game. They were in it long before I came on the scene. Being in boxing is a thankless job. However, there is a job to be done and we must make a go of it. I am running our business the only way I can see to conduct it. If the government tells us that our way is wrong we will have to find another way. Maybe we can't operate another way, maybe we can't operate at all, if the present system is considered illegal."

●　　●　　●

Ray Robinson, in late 1954, announced to the world that his retirement from boxing was over. After being away from the sport since his loss to Joey Maxim in the extreme heat at Yankee Stadium on June 24, 1952, he was returning to boxing. His show business career as a song-and-dance man in night clubs had slowed down, not creating the type of income he was accustomed to making as a professional boxer. Robinson began to work out at his training camp in Greenwood Lakes, a short drive from Broadway and his offices at Ray Robinson Enterprises in Harlem.

Sugar Ray was determined to get back to the level of competence he was at when he left boxing in 1952. He approached his comeback in earnest, mindful of the challenge that lay ahead. Other great champions of the past had attempted to return to the ring after a prolonged absence, with mixed results. The great Benny Leonard had retired as the undefeated lightweight champion in 1924. Five years later, the stock market crash had wiped out most of his wealth, forcing him to come back to boxing, this time as a welterweight. He took on welterweight champion Jimmy McLarnin, who stopped him in six rounds. Leonard, following his one-sided defeat, realized his days as a quality fighter were over and retired for good.

In 1910, Jim Jeffries returned to fight Jack Johnson for the heavyweight title after a six-year layoff. Jeffries, pressured into a comeback by a white America that did not appreciate a Negro boxer holding the crown, was a shell of his former self. Jeffries was KO'd in the fifteenth round, soundly beaten by Johnson throughout the fight.

Closer to home, the unsuccessful return of Joe Louis to boxing also preyed on Sugar Ray's mind, the memory of rushing to the ring apron back in 1951, distraught as he comforted Louis, who lay motionless after being knocked out by Rocky Marciano. He recalled how he cried at the sight of his dear friend lying there, promising himself that he would never let that happen to him.

One of the biggest concerns that a boxer has in returning to fighting is their legs, which lose their resiliency from inactivity. Fortunately for Sugar Ray, that was not a problem because of his "show biz" career as a tap dancer. Robinson worried that he would be thirty-four years old the following May and wondered how his aging body would respond to the physical aspects of boxing. Also, was his heart still in it? He never liked the sport but still managed to get himself up for training and matches. He thought his battery had been recharged after being away from boxing for three years, but he wouldn't be sure until he gave it a go. The memories of the Maxim fight and the pain and horror of almost dying all came back to him. He again was reminded of the tremendous toll boxing had taken on his body. He liked the money boxing provided, giving him the liquid cash he needed. It was his life. He liked the trappings that came along with being champion. He liked people around him calling him "Champ," but that took money. He was financially strapped, with the IRS again hounding him for back taxes. A return to the ring could solve those problems. He knew he was pushing the envelope coming back, but it had to be done—he was a fighter. It was what he did better than anyone else. He needed boxing, and boxing needed him.

Robinson's training went well enough to be able to schedule his first fight in Detroit on January 5, 1955. His opponent was a former marine from Roxbury, Massachusetts, Joe Rindone. In the sixth round Robinson knocked Rindone out with a textbook left-right combination. The crowd of twelve thousand at the Olympia roared its approval as Sugar Ray made a successful return to professional boxing. In the dressing room afterward, Robinson was not pleased with his performance. He thought he should have knocked his opponent out sooner, referring to him as the ugliest fighter he had ever fought. Rindone, for his part, had kept a streak of his own alive: it was the fourth time in four straight fights that he had been knocked out.

Sugar Ray, following the Rindone fight, was aware that he still had a lot of work to do if he was to get back to the level he was at in the early 1950s. His goal, by ending his retirement from boxing, was to make money, money that came only from fighting for championships, and he was not at that level yet. Two weeks later, on January 19 in Chicago, Tiger Jones confirmed Robinson's concerns, soundly beating him over ten rounds.

ARTHUR DALEY (Writer): "He was not the Robinson of old, but an old Robinson."

JIMMY CANNON (Writer): "Robinson at one time was a marvelous boxer . . . he isn't anymore. That's no disgrace either. The years did it to him and not Tiger Jones."

Sugar Ray was so disappointed over the loss to Tiger Jones that it took him weeks to mentally recover from the defeat. His rock, George Gainford, had walked away from Robinson after the fight, convinced his friend was washed up. Fortunately, Robinson's wife, Edna Mae, intervened and put the two back together. She convinced each man that together they could still achieve greatness. She scolded Gainford for his lack of faith in Sugar Ray while softly suggesting to her husband that he get back to boxing instead of trying to knock everyone out.

Sugar Ray decided his wife was right, and he began once again focusing on his boxing skills. He realized that in his rush to get back to the top, he had tried to make a statement by knocking out his opponents rather than boxing them. He would concentrate on using all his wondrous skills in the ring and no longer concern himself with knockouts.

The change back to his more effective style of fighting quickly brought results, as he reeled off four straight wins. Now convinced he was ready to fight for a championship, a match was arranged with Bobo Olsen, the middleweight champion of the world. The fight would take place in Chicago, the site where Tiger Jones had taken him apart less than eleven months earlier. Robinson had come a long way since that loss. Olsen would be fighting a different Ray Robinson than Tiger Jones had faced. Once again it was like old times for Sugar Ray, in the spotlight fighting for a title. It was a good feeling to be back.

Ray Robinson trained hard for his third fight with Bobo Olsen. The first two encounters had gone Sugar Ray's way, knocking Bobo out in 1950, then by a decision two years later in San Francisco. Each fighter had something to prove going into this middleweight title fight, with the loser's career as a top fighter in jeopardy. A convincing win by either fighter would silence the critics. The stakes would be high on December 9, 1955, when they met at center ring. This upcoming bout would be the thirteenth time Sugar Ray had fought for a championship . . . He hoped it would be his "Lucky 13."

Bobo Olsen, since winning the middleweight crown in 1953, had successfully defended his title three times, with decisive wins over welterweight king Kid Gavilan, Rocky Castellani, and Pierre Langlois. After beating Joey Maxim, he decided to try for the light heavyweight crown worn by Archie Moore. They fought in September 1955, at the Polo Grounds, with Moore knocking Bobo out in the third round. Olsen, the notoriously slow starter, had fought a smart fight through the first two rounds, jabbing at Moore and staying out of range of his powerful punching power. In the third round both fighters were in close, whaling away at each other, when Moore stepped back, loaded up, and caught Olsen with a left hook that stopped Bobo in his tracks. As Olsen's body headed for the canvas, Moore hit him with another left hook and a right hand high on his balding head, ending his evening.

The Hawaiian-born fighter needed to bounce back with a solid fight against Robinson. At thirty-one years old, he was in his eleventh year as a professional boxer. He went into the fight a 3-1 favorite to beat Robinson, but most fight experts believed he needed to survive the first five rounds before having a legitimate chance of winning. The longer the fight went on, the better Bobo's chances were to win. If the fight ended early, Robinson probably had knocked him out.

•　　•　　•

CHICAGO, DECEMBER 9, 1955. On a cold crisp night in Chicago, a disappointing crowd of 12,441 fans showed up at the Chicago Stadium to watch Olsen and Robinson renew hostilities. The champion moved inside from the opening bell, hoping to physically wear down his older opponent. Robinson, fully prepared for these tactics, allowed Olsen to lead, then counterpunched effectively throughout the first round. In the second round Olsen again tried to move inside, but Sugar Ray each time peppered him with well-timed combinations. Olsen, becoming frustrated, tried to bully his way inside but was hit by a Robinson right hand, followed by a left hook and an equally fast right cross that sent him plunging to the canvas. Bobo, as the count reached eight, tried to get up but fell back, his days as middleweight champion over. Sugar Ray Robinson had come all the way back, defying the odds, proving his critics wrong. He was back in the catbird seat, the best fighter in his weight class. It felt special to a very special fighter.

SUGAR RAY ROBINSON (Boxer): "I had to cry. I just couldn't believe it was all over. This comeback has been a *'ghost of a thing,'* with me ever since Tiger Jones licked me here in Chicago Stadium. Only a few people thought I should continue after that and to them I owe thanks. But many others said I didn't have a chance, that I should quit for good. It was a very hard thing to swallow and very hard getting ready to continue."

There was a rematch clause within ninety days, but IBC president James Norris would not confer where the fourth Robinson-Olsen fight would take place. Bobo said after the fight that he welcomed another shot at his nemesis.

BOBO OLSEN (Boxer): "So fast, so fast. It was his fast combinations and I got careless. It was too fast. I don't know, maybe the referee counted too fast. Did he? I'll fight him again. Those combinations stunned me, they were so fast and I got careless. The first round went just like I wanted it to . . . he didn't hurt me at all . . . but that second round was bullshit. He hit me hard but not as hard as Archie Moore."

Sid Flaherty, Bobo Olsen's manager, pointed to family troubles as part of the reason for Bobo's recent poor performances. Olsen's wife had filed for divorce in their hometown of San Francisco.

Sugar Ray said he would honor the ninety-day rematch and would allow Olsen more time if he needed it to straighten out his marital problems. Sugar Ray Robinson said the day after the fight that as far as he was concerned, Bobo could have the repeat fight anytime he wanted.

SUGAR RAY ROBINSON (Boxer): "I know he's having family trouble and I hope he patches things up quickly."

The victory was so one-sided for Sugar Ray that he refused to allow any financial difficulties to take away from his enjoyment of becoming the middleweight champion again. Other than the Tiger Jones loss, it had been a triumphant return to boxing. He inwardly took great pride in what he had accomplished, especially when people close to him thought it was not possible. The year 1955 had been very special, and he looked forward to 1956. He would defend his title a few more times before retiring for good and going back into show business. He doubted he would be in the sport more than a couple of years.

•   •   •

The welterweight championship fight between Carmen Basilio and Tony DeMarco at the Onondaga County War Memorial had been sold out for weeks. Because the fight was being blacked out within a hundred-mile radius of Syracuse, promoter Norm Rothschild installed two large television screens at the nearby New York State Fairgrounds to provide additional seating. Local taverns, throughout the week, were installing antennas on their roofs to pick up a Kingston, Ontario, television station that was carrying the broadcast in Canada. The local Haberle Brewing Company placed a television in the window of its Butternut Street store, where people would be able to walk up and watch the bout. Everywhere you went in Syracuse, people were talking about "the fight." This time around, Basilio was favored to win, and Syracuse was bracing for its first champion in a long time. The area had not had a champion since Babe Risko won the middleweight title in 1935. It was a bit ironic that two mobsters, Gabe Genovese and Frankie Carbo, had a hand in both championships, first as managers of Risko and then as facilitators of the fight in 1955.

Tony DeMarco came into the fight riding a sixteen-fight unbeaten streak. A draw against lightweight champ Jimmy Carter in February 1955 was the closest he had come to losing. Some critics scoffed at him being welterweight champion when he couldn't decisively defeat the lightweight champion. Regardless, this dynamo from Boston's Little Italy was a tough customer.

AUSTIN LAKE (Writer): "Don't sell this boy [DeMarco] short on courage nor desire. He's every bit as hungry and determined as Basilio. He's got the championship and he wants more than anything in the world to keep it. If he gets hurt he'll not quit. He'll fight all the harder."

The champion flew into Syracuse a day before the fight after completing his training at Kutchner's Camp in the Catskill Mountains. Basilio finished his training in Syracuse at Robbins Gym. Both fighters, always in great condition, had to be slowed down by their handlers, who were concerned about them becoming stale. Basilio, five years older than DeMarco at twenty-eight years old, would go into the fight at 145½ pounds, an advantage of three-quarters of a pound. Basilio had waited two long years for this chance after being passed over time and time again by fighters who were ranked below him. He knew he had to make the most of this opportunity. Time was running out for his dream of becoming a champion.

ARCHIE MOORE: "I've seen Basilio fight and he's a great little fighter. He has earned a chance to fight for the Title and I am glad to see him get it."

AUSTIN LAKE (Writer): "DeMarco is a good counter-puncher. I believe he will hit Basilio often. Basilio is a trader. A Dempsey-like guy who is willing to take a couple to land one of his own. I suspect that Basilio does more damage with his punches than does DeMarco. In other words he doesn't turn over as much stock, but he pays bigger dividends when he does."

•   •   •

SYRACUSE, JUNE 10, 1955. More than nine thousand fans jammed Syracuse's War Memorial, paying between three dollars for a general admission ticket to twenty dollars for a ringside ducat. Both fighters, from the opening bell, fought as expected, relentlessly attacking each other as their fists flew fast and often. Each, so similar in style, attitude, and desire, never backed away from this human endurance contest. Basilio, as planned, went to the champion's midsection, slamming him round after round with lethal body blows. DeMarco countered with his own form of warfare, staggering Basilio in the third with a hard left hand, opening a gash over his right eye. DeMarco moved in but couldn't put Basilio away as the bell rang. In the seventh round, DeMarco reopened the cut above Basilio's eye, but the challenger, unfazed, blasted away inside, with combinations to the champion's body.

The fight began to turn in Basilio's favor as it reached the ninth round. DeMarco, feeling the effects of Basilio's punches, began to tire. Sensing that he was running out of gas, DeMarco went head-hunting, swinging wildly, trying to knock Basilio out. After a couple of misguided punches missed their mark, DeMarco slumped to the canvas, his legs giving out. Beating the count, the game champion hung on but took a vicious beating the remainder of the round. In the tenth round Basilio decked DeMarco twice, but the champion fought on, refusing to give in. Somehow, DeMarco answered the bell in the twelfth, slowly edging toward Basilio, his hands high, his face awash with blood. His energy now sapped, his championship in peril, DeMarco refused to give in. He was not going to relinquish the title he was so proud of. He would not quit.

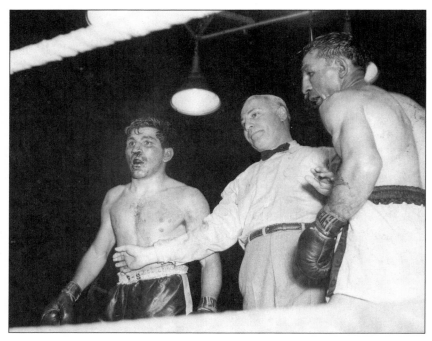

23. Basilio-DeMarco fight of June 10, 1955. *(Left to right):* Tony DeMarco, the referee, and Carmen Basilio. *Courtesy of Carmen Basilio.*

Basilio met him at center ring, where he closed in to finish off his battered opponent. He hit DeMarco with left-right combinations that signaled the end, as the referee stepped in, ending this epic battle between two great competitors.

Carmen Basilio had achieved his dream: he was welterweight champion of the world. Carmen, overcome by emotion, collapsed to the canvas, tears running down his face. His mother, Mary, was led to the center of the ring, where she embraced him, sharing this special moment with her grateful son. Standing by Carmen's corner, dressed in a suit and tie, his father, Joseph, looked on with pride—an immigrant from Italy, the father of the welterweight champion of the world, his dreams too had been fulfilled.

The deposed champion was led back to his dressing room as the Syracuse fans erupted in applause for this courageous man's efforts. Two years before they had jeered Kid Gavilan, but tonight they had only respect for the effort and determination of Tony DeMarco. Back in Boston, people were preparing signs that would be displayed on DeMarco's return home, showing their love and support for him.

JACK SLATTERY (Writer): "If ever fans should be proud of a loser, it should be DeMarco fans. He was down twice. What brought him to his feet and out for the twelfth round only DeMarco will know. It was both thrilling and terrifying to see him fight from pure instinct. At the end of the tenth and eleventh round the game lad walked blindly into the television lights directly opposite his corner."

DAN FLORIO (DeMarco Cutman): "I wish the kid never landed that left hand in the third round. It buckled Basilio's knees and from that time he was left hook, one-punch kayo crazy. We couldn't get him to stop after that."

CARMEN BASILIO: "I know a left really sent him spinning at the end of the 10th, but actually I feel that the fight was won before that. During the eighth I tagged him often and hard in the mid-section and in the ninth he slowed to a walk. That was it. He couldn't move out of range and I was able to shorten my shots. Believe me, Tony is an underrated fighter. He hurt me real bad in the first round, but the blow that seemed to shake me up in the third, didn't hurt at all."

ANGELO DUNDEE (Basilio Cornerman): "This kid [Basilio] is the strongest welterweight in the sport and what a guy to work with in a corner. He makes us all look like brain-busters. He does every single thing we tell him and never disagrees or second guesses."

Johnny DeJohn, following his fighter winning the welterweight title, wanted a second fight with DeMarco in Boston. He knew it would do big business because he saw firsthand the tremendous following DeMarco had there when he fought Johnny Saxton. DeJohn got in touch with Blinky Palermo because his fighter had the contract to fight the winner of the Basilio-DeMarco match. Saxton desperately wanted the fight, as did Palermo. Johnny said to

Blinky, "Listen, why don't you let Carmen fight DeMarco again and then you fight the winner. In the meantime, we can give you some money out of this deal. This is going to draw a lot of money." Palermo said, "We'll wait." Blinky made an easy ten thousand dollars for letting the DeMarco-Basilio second fight happen.

DONNIE HAMILTON (Boxing Historian): "Johnny protected Carmen. He always looked out for his interests while making a buck for himself. In those days, most of the managers got 50 percent, but they paid all the expenses. Carmen paid Johnny and Joe one-third, and whatever came out for the New York people came out of their end. It never came out of Carmen's end."

ROSS STAGNITTI: "Moments after Carmen Basilio stopped Tony DeMarco to win the welterweight title in Syracuse [June 10, 1955], the new champ had a craving for orange juice. My father, Joe Stagnitti, exited the Onondaga County War Memorial in search of the requested refreshment. After purchasing the juice at a local tavern, Dad returned but was stopped by a police officer. Carmen's trainer, Angelo Dundee, opened the dressing room door and told Dad to wait outside for Carmen as he reached for the juice. Determined to congratulate his hometown hero, Dad emphatically stated that he would personally deliver it to Carmen. His persistence paid off. As he poured the juice, the moment was captured in a photo. Fifty years later to the day, Dad re-created that moment by bringing orange juice to Carmen at Fight Night during the 2005 Hall of Fame Induction Weekend."

•   •   •

BOSTON, NOVEMBER 30, 1955. A crowd of 13,373 crammed into Boston Garden to watch the second installment of the Carmen Basilio versus Tony DeMarco wars. It had been just 173 days since DeMarco had lost his championship to Basilio in Syracuse. This time around he'd be fighting before the home crowd, and he was primed not to disappoint them. The champion was an early 7-5 favorite to defend his title, but as the fight neared it became a 6-5 you-pick-'em.

24. Juice for the champ. *(Left to right):* Armondo Basilio, Joey Basilio, Paul Basilio, Carmen Basilio, Joe Stagnitti, and Carmen's father, Joseph. *Courtesy of Carmen Basilio.*

Tony DeMarco came out storming against Basilio, this time constantly moving in and out, beating his aggressive opponent to the punch. The challenger bombed Basilio from all angles with carefully constructed jabs, uppercuts, and hooks to the body. Focusing more this time on boxing his opponent versus the quick knockout, he clearly controlled the action, rocking Basilio in the fourth with a solid right hand that staggered the champion. DeMarco remained on the attack through rounds five and six.

Late in the seventh round, DeMarco delivered a series of combinations to the head that dazed Basilio, causing the champion to wobble backward again in trouble. Rubber-legged, defenseless, Basilio was on the verge of being knocked down for only the second time in sixty-six fights. DeMarco bore in, flailing at the champion as the highly partisan Boston crowd roared him on. Most fighters would have gone down under the barrage of punches thrown by DeMarco, but that intangible that separates fighters, that toughness all champions have, surfaced, and Basilio somehow survived the round. Angelo Dundee worked feverishly between rounds to revive a stunned Basilio while challenging him to step it up. "Carmen, that guy's got your title unless you go to the belly. Let's go, pick it up."

In the opposite corner DeMarco sat in disbelief that Basilio had not gone down. He had exerted a tremendous amount of energy to end the fight, but somehow the resolve of Carmen Basilio had prevented him from completing the job. He wondered what it was going to take to defeat this man. What he had just administered to Basilio should have knocked him out. The demons of self-doubt crept into his psyche, but DeMarco again pushed them aside and went back at Basilio when the bell rang. DeMarco forced the action throughout the next three minutes, but the tide began to turn in the ninth toward the champion. Basilio somehow summoned the strength to surge back against a tiring Tony DeMarco and began to take control of the match. He attacked DeMarco's midsection as Dundee had advised, with viscous combinations that punch by punch knocked the life out of the game challenger. DeMarco tried to stop Basilio's onslaught by grabbing and holding the craggy-faced champion, but Basilio kept the pressure on, finally knocking him down early in the twelfth round. DeMarco, bleeding and physically drained, beat the count, but Basilio was waiting for him and hit him with a blistering four-punch combination "bam-bam-bam-bam," and down went DeMarco as referee Mel Manning moved in to stop the fight at 1:54. This second match had lasted just two seconds longer than their first encounter.

These two great fighters had fought an epic battle of determination and grit. Tony DeMarco, bleeding from the mouth and cut above both eyes, had refused to quit, although his beaten body had no more to give. Carmen Basilio, it was learned after the fight, had broken his left hand in the second round. Deprived of his major weapon, the left hook, he fought on, forced to occasionally throw it despite the agonizing pain it caused him.

Basilio kept the crown that night in Boston, but these two men would be joined at the hip, as part of the famous "Bloodbath in Boston," still considered one of the greatest fights in boxing history. *Ring Magazine* voted it the "Fight of the Year," nudging their first fight in Syracuse the previous June to second place. This would be the last time these two great warriors would meet in the ring, but a friendship was forged from the respect each had developed for the other.

The champion earned $74,490 for his efforts, which came to 40 percent and included the radio and television fees. DeMarco received $37,245 for his share.

IBC president James Norris, in attendance, said that a match with Johnny Saxton was being discussed, with possible sites being Chicago, Miami, San Francisco, or Syracuse. Saxton's manager, Blinky Palermo, had lost his licence in New York, which could prevent Syracuse from getting another title bout. Regardless, the new champion would need some well-deserved time off to allow his left hand to heal.

CARMEN BASILIO: "After the seventh round, when he hurt me I could see that he was getting tired and it was a question of time until he ran out of gas."

DONNIE HAMILTON (Boxing Historian): "When Carmen fought Tony DeMarco in Boston, the place was packed. You talk about an environment of a fight—everybody was betting. On every corner, in the arena, everybody was laying some money down. When Carmen got hit in the seventh, I wouldn't give you a dime for Carmen surviving that fight. People were still betting. They were betting Carmen wouldn't make it. The Boston people loved Tony DeMarco. After the round, when the warning buzzer rang, Carmen got up, and he's stomping his feet. I remember turning to someone and saying, 'Carmen's okay. He's a hotheaded Italian, he's mad, and he wants to get back in the fight.' Well, that really wasn't the case. The fight goes on, and Carmen wins the fight. I'm talking to Carmen after the fight, and I asked him if he was mad after that round. He said that wasn't the case at all. 'My legs were numb. I was trying to get the circulation going.' That's how hard he was hit, yet he still came back and won. He broke a lot of good fighters' hearts because they would hit him with everything, and this guy's still coming."

●   ●   ●

On December 12, 1955, the New York State Athletic Commission announced that any member of the Managers' Guild who did not resign from the guild by January 16, 1956, would have their license revoked. Julius Helfand, in delivering the ultimatum, accused the guild of engaging in "vague and shadowy activities, of actions that were malevolent, monopolistic, flagrant, vicious, shocking, arbitrary and illegal, absolute and autocratic, underhanded and dishonest." He accused guild members of consorting with the "sinister and shadowy figure" of the notorious Frankie Carbo and, what was worse, displaying incredible ignorance of their own organization. It became crystal clear that this commissioner was on a mission to clean up boxing in New York. The guild quickly responded to the edict, saying that its members were united in this fight and would fight back in court if necessary. One guild member thought Helfand should give them more time. *"If it took Helfand six-months to make a decision, how did he expect a bunch of dumb guys to make a decision in three minutes?"*

25. Carmen Basilio and Johnny Saxton square off in Chicago, March 14, 1956. *Courtesy of Ada Rothschild.*

10.

Chicago Justice

the sport of boxing in April 1956 lost one of its great champions, as Rocky Marciano announced his retirement. The Brockton, Massachusetts, native, undefeated in forty-nine fights, forty-three by knockout, said that his decision was final. Following his impressive knockout of Archie Moore in September 1955, it became one of the best unkept secrets in boxing that Marciano was looking to get out. Throughout his career he had approached his training with a Spartan-like attitude, which according to Rocky had taken its toll on his body. Also, he was tired of dealing with his manager, Al Weill, who, while adroitly handling his career, dominated him in a way that at times was demeaning to him. Weill, when asked a few months before about a rumor that Marciano was considering retirement, responded in his usual caustic manner: *"Marciano will quit . . . when I tell him to quit."*

Rocky Marciano had nothing left to prove in the ring. There were no real "big money" opponents left to fight. The ageless Archie Moore was the last heavyweight challenger that the public wanted to see fight, with most of the prefight hype created by Moore himself. A youthful Floyd Patterson was coming on the scene, creating a buzz, but he wasn't the drawing card he would become in the next few years. All in all, Rocky was choosing a good time to depart. His unblemished record was still intact, and he was going out on his terms, with his adoring public grudgingly supportive of his decision.

CHARLEY GOLDMAN (Rocky Marciano's Trainer): "Rocky when he first started with me was in the ring with this fella and I couldn't stop from laughing watching him fight. Once he was backed against the ropes and he put both of his hands up over his head and just leaned back while the other fella hit him a mile a minute. I stopped it and asked Rocky what he was doing, and he told me, 'The fellows who taught me to fight always said that when a guy got me against the ropes I should put my hands over my head and let him hit me in the belly until he got tired and then I should clout him on top of the head and knock him out.' I had to take a walk down to the other end of the gym when I heard that, but when I told them to fight again, Rocky hit this other fellow with a right hand which nearly put a hole in the guy's head and I knew that something could be done with this boy."

•   •   •

Carmen Basilio basked in the glory of being the welterweight champion in 1956. His fight with Tony DeMarco was voted the "Fight of the Year" in 1955, and a *Ring Magazine* fan poll rated him the sport's most popular fighter. All the work, all the disappointments over the past few years, had been worth it. He had climbed to the top of his weight class, earning his way step by step, rung by rung. He was a proud champion.

Basilio's first title defense would be against Johnny Saxton in Chicago in March 1956. Blinky Palermo, Saxton's manager, was not licensed in New York, which prevented their fight from happening in Syracuse or Madison Square Garden. Chicago became the obvious choice for the IBC, staging the fight at the Chicago Stadium. The Windy City had not been kind to Carmen Basilio, but the confident champion didn't concern himself with past history. His relationship with the IBC had improved, and he believed he would be treated fairly. If James Norris wanted him to fight in Chicago, then that is where he would fight.

CARMEN BASILIO: "Mr. Norris is a gentleman and a man of his word. If it wasn't for Mr. Norris I wouldn't have been

Champion. He's given me the opportunity to put myself where I am today."

* * *

The New York State Athletic Commission's decision in December 1955 had put all International Boxing Guild members on notice that if they still belonged to the organization after January 16, 1956, they would run the risk of their license being suspended. A few of the guild's leaders had tried to circumvent the commission's edict by moving some fights out of state. Others hoped that the powerful IBC would move its headquarters to Chicago, while shifting boxing matches scheduled for Madison Square Garden to Illinois or Michigan. The members hoped this action would force the commission to soften its position regarding the guild.

Julius Helfand understood that if progress was to be made in the cleanup of boxing in New York, he would need the support of James Norris. The International Boxing Club's president had to be on board. The only real choice the guild had at the moment was to move fights away from New York or disband. If the powerful Jim Norris became Helfand's ally in this battle, it would break the guild, and the cleanup of the fight game in New York would continue. If he did not have the IBC's support, then the commission's position would be weakened and down the road possibly compromised. Helfand had to convince Jim Norris to turn his back on the guild and join his team. This would be no easy task, considering the pressure Norris was receiving from the guild members and their new best friend, Frankie Carbo.

A meeting was arranged at Helfand's office with Norris ten days prior to the guild's deadline going into effect. Norris, as expected, told Helfand that he was reluctant to go against the guild, afraid that he would have difficulty filling his Madison Square Garden fight cards. Helfand dismissed that reasoning, angrily reminding Norris that he had always proclaimed to be a proponent of cleaning up boxing. Helfand demanded that Norris do the right thing, regardless of his fears about the guild boycotting his fights. Norris countered, saying he would support the ruling but only if another guild could be formed to take its place. Helfand, furious with that suggestion, lit into Norris, telling the IBC president that under no circumstances would that be allowed. He closed his appeal by telling Norris that he was either for cleaning up boxing or he was not. The position he took would determine that.

Jim Norris knew he was over a barrel. There was no way he could satisfy both parties on this decision. If he didn't side with Helfand, then his integrity would be in question. He always publicly stated he was for what was best for boxing. Going against the New York State Athletic Commission's decree, he knew, was not in the best interests of boxing. But going against the guild was not a good business decision, either. The "rubber met the road" in Norris's mind as he considered his options. The aggressive Julius Helfand was not going to allow him a pass on this one. He would be forced to take an unpopular position. Wealthy men, like James Norris, never have to publicly make unpopular decisions . . . that's what they pay others to do. He was caught, and he knew it. There was really only one option for James D. Norris, and it had nothing to do with boxing.

The end came swiftly to the guild when James Norris said that the IBC was supporting the New York State Athletic Commission. Only a few hard-core managers refused to resign from an organization that, in reality, no longer existed. Julius Helfand was being credited with taking down a part of this monster that was destroying boxing. A clear message was sent out that this "good ole boy" mentality, where individuals could do whatever they damn well pleased, was over in New York. Managers who wanted to work in an honest, aboveboard manner would be welcome, but those who preferred a coercive style of business would be asked to leave. There would begin to be some accountability to the fight game in the Empire State, as the tide began to turn against the old guard. The Mob still had Chicago to exact their illicit influence in, but they were being put on notice that their days were numbered. The federal government was about to be heard, as its hearings would begin in April.

Julius Helfand understood that there would always be work to do in order to clean up boxing because of the nature of the business. The sport always had a way of drawing the "shysters" and "crooks" to it, those looking for an easy buck—and that would never change. The best part of boxing was between the ropes; that's why the sport had survived all these years. Helfand's decree had merely gotten the ball rolling, and it would be up to the Justice Department and the courts to eliminate organized crime from boxing.

NAT FLEISCHER (Editor, *Ring Magazine*): "The sport can be referred to as the 'Sport of Rogues.' Although there were some honest promoters when I began covering the sport in the 1930's, boxing as a whole was run by ruffians, gangsters and politicians."

JULIUS HELFAND: "I'm not a promoter of boxing, nor am I a matchmaker. I am an administrator of the laws under which boxing exists in New York."

• • •

John DeJohn was so pleased with his fighter's workouts leading up to the fight against Johnny Saxton that he told the press that Basilio had never looked better. DeJohn wanted this fight to be up close and personal.

JOHN DEJOHN: "Our guy is a better fighter right now than he's ever been. I sure hope he stays this way. I have never seen Carmen look this good in my life. I always hoped for him to be great, and even though he became champion, it did not mean he became a great fighter. But today and in other recent workouts, Carmen has done things he has never done before. The things I hoped to see in him . . . I saw today. I definitely believe that Basilio is at his peak right now. He's a much better fighter than when he fought Tony DeMarco. I hope I'm not jinxing Carmen. I felt this way once before when my brother Joey fought, and he got knocked out."

Many people were puzzled that Basilio would choose to make his first title defense in Chicago. Things always seemed to go against him there. It appeared to be an odd choice of venues for the welterweight champion. He bristled at the mention of him making a mistake taking the fight to Chicago. "That was before I won the title. I didn't come here to be beaten," an agitated Basilio told the press.

The progress Basilio was making as a fighter also amazed many of the Chicago boxing writers who attended his workouts. He looked so different from the guy who had lost to Chuck Davey a few years before. He was a much stronger puncher. His two twelve-round knockouts of Tony DeMarco demonstrated the cumulative effect of his punching. He wore DeMarco down to the point that Tony collapsed. Adding the additional five rounds in a championship fight benefited the supremely conditioned Basilio. He wasn't going to knock a guy out with one punch, but his midbody punching prowess would eventually take its toll. He thrived in fifteen-round competition. The hospitality and warmth directed toward him prior to the match made Basilio feel that his fight with Saxton would go off without a hitch. The challenger had other ideas about how this fight would be fought.

JOHNNY SAXTON: "I won't make the same mistake I made against Tony DeMarco. I won't try to out-bang a banger. I know Carmen Basilio hits harder than I do, so I will give him a boxing lesson. Of course, I won't pass up any good openings to let him have it."

Johnny Saxton was an excellent defensive boxer whose counterpunching abilities were as good as there was in boxing in the mid-1950s. His jab effectively set up his combinations to an opponent's head or body. He seemed to fight better against aggressive-type fighters, those who liked to attack. They played into his counterpunching talents. Since Blinky Palermo took over his career and replaced his teacher and trainer, Bill Miller, he had not been the same fighter. Miller had helped him between rounds, and Saxton always responded to his suggestions. Now he was more on his own, and at times it showed in his performance—boxing fans were never sure which fighter would show up to fight.

CARMEN BASILIO: "As a fighter, I've never been better and I am not so smart that I stop learning. I learn something every day in the gym and being Champ makes you fight that much harder. They can't come any harder than Tony DeMarco."

*   *   *

CHICAGO, MARCH 14, 1956. Carmen Basilio came out in the first round as he had predicted, attacking Johnny Saxton, pummeling him with left-right combinations to the body. Saxton, fighting defensively, countered Basilio by peppering him with jabs, but the champion cleverly ducked underneath, slamming a right to the body and a hook to the head. Basilio kept the aggression up throughout the round, with most writers believing Basilio had won the first round. Unfortunately for Basilio, that didn't take into account the two officials and referee who all awarded the first round to Saxton. Basilio again was the busier fighter in the second round, as he continued to attack the challenger, who now began to grab and hold, doing far more wrestling than boxing. In the third round Saxton's glove ripped, causing the stuffing to come out. His bare thumbnail scraped along Basilio's eyelid, causing it to bleed. The fight was halted until another glove was located, giving each fighter a ten-minute rest. When the match resumed, Johnny Saxton continued to grab and hold Basilio, which forced referee Frank Gilmer to constantly step between the fighters and separate them. This frustrated Basilio because it broke up the rhythm of the fight, and it prevented him from being able to fight inside. Each time he positioned himself for some inside body punching, Gilmer would step between him and Saxton. This pattern continued without interruption throughout the remainder of the fight.

In Basilio's corner, John DeJohn couldn't believe what he was witnessing. The referee, in his mind, was preventing Basilio from fighting his fight. There was no way the champion could get at the challenger. Fighting from a distance was working in Saxton's favor, which meant that the outcome of the fight would be determined by the two officials and referee. That was not something the Basilio camp wanted or planned for. They expected Carmen to knock Saxton out.

When the decision was announced, Johnny Saxton was unanimously judged to be the winner of the fight. The Chicago Stadium crowd of 12,145 booed the decision. Saxton, for the second time, it appeared, had been given the welterweight title that most observers believed he hadn't won. Nineteen out of the twenty-five writers polled after the fight thought Basilio had won the fight. It appeared to people around boxing that "Chicago justice" had been served by the toughest of enforcers, Frankie Carbo. His henchman, Blinky Palermo, had been handsomely paid back for waiting to have his fighter get another crack at the welterweight crown.

Because the fight was in Illinois, it was scored on a point system. One judge scored it 145 to 138. The other judge had it 147 to 140, and the referee, Frank Gilmer, had it the closest, at 142 to 140, all seeing Saxton as the winner. The crowd expressed its displeasure for the decision for more than ten minutes. There was no provision in the contract for a repeat fight. Carmen Basilio, who had been unfairly passed over time and time again for a title shot, appeared to be on the outside looking in once more.

CARMEN BASILIO: "I always thought that the challenger had to take it away from the champion big. I know he didn't do that. That referee didn't help me. He's the same guy who had me here with Chuck Davey and he did the same thing when we were punching in close. He broke it up. He took away one of the better weapons I had when he wouldn't allow me to punch on the inside. Saxton never hurt me. No never. He can't punch with DeMarco. He's not anything like him. He just jabbed and ran. His only aim was to stay there for fifteen rounds. He never tried to make a fight of it."

JOHNNY SAXTON: "Carmen Basilio is the strongest boy I have fought. He's durable. There was no holding him off, he just kept coming all the time. Now, I would like a chance at the winner between Sugar Ray Robinson and Bobo Olsen."

An hour later, sitting alone in his dressing room, his head down, Basilio slowly pounded his aching left fist into the palm of his equally sore right hand, replaying the fight. The deposed champion could not understand why boxing had to be this way. He had worked so hard in preparation for his first title defense. Titles should be won, not decided by people who have other interests in mind.

CARMEN BASILIO: "They stole my Title . . . that referee gave me the worst of it. He wouldn't let me fight inside, he kept breaking us apart. I'll never fight in Chicago again. Now, I have to start over."

JOHN DEJOHN: "It's now up to the International Boxing Club and the writers to get Carmen back in the ring with Saxton. It is the newsmen who form the opinion."

DAN PARKER (Writer): "How much ability and popular appeal mean to the IBC and its wire pullers can be seen when a fine, honest, popular fighter like Basilio is sacrificed to get Saxton, boxing's number 1 arena stinker, back on the throne. Basilio has never appeared in a bad fight. The honesty of his efforts has never been questioned. He and Rocky Marciano are the boxers in whom the public has unlimited confidence."

JESS ABRAMSON (Writer): "Do you know of a worse decision in a championship fight? The Saxton win over Gavilan in Philadelphia was bad, but nothing to compare with this."

The next day a smiling Johnny Saxton picked up a check for $42,677. Earlier in the day Saxton had received a call from Jim Norris, who suggested that he give Basilio a repeat fight, sometime in early summer. Norris knew the decision didn't lie in Saxton's lap. Those decisions were decided by his manager, Blinky Palermo, and Frankie Carbo. Norris, feeling the heat from the press, had to get another Saxton-Basilio fight scheduled or at least have the appearance that they were in some type of negotiations. Arranging another Basilio-Saxton fight in Chicago would be a tough sell to the press and the public. Norris knew after consoling the distraught Basilio after the fight that Carmen wanted a rematch as soon as possible, preferably in New York. The IBC president would need the help of Julius Helfand to make that happen. He had helped Helfand destroy the Managers' Guild . . . It was now time for Helfand to help him.

• • •

On April 26, 1956, in the U.S. District Court of New York, Judge Sylvester J. Ryan presided over the case between the plaintiff, the United States of America, and the defendants, the IBC of New York, Inc.; the IBC of Illinois, Inc.; Madison Square Garden Corporation; James D. Norris; and Arthur M. Wirtz. William J. Elkins represented the government, while Whitney North Seymour was the chief defense counsel.

WILLIAM J. ELKINS (Department of Justice): "This case presents classic instances of violations of anti-trust laws. A group of men have banded together to seek domination of a field. In this they have succeeded. It is submitted that the equity powers of this Court should be invoked to dissolve that amalgamation of powers and to enjoin the illegal practices through which it was achieved."

The government called eight witnesses to testify, each solidifying the position that James Norris's and Arthur Wirtz's actions and the interweaving corporations they represented acted in a monopolistic way. The most powerful testimony came from fight promoters, who told of being required to share receipts off the top in order to obtain top fighters who had signed personal service contracts with the IBC. Near the close of the government hearings, General John Reed Kilpatrick was called to the stand. The tall, distinguished honorary chairman of the Madison Square Garden Corporation had throughout his chairmanship kept a very organized diary of all his correspondence and personal meetings. The general had in his possession a letter that Arthur Wirtz had written to him in March 1949, expressing his concerns regarding the direction of boxing at Madison Square Garden under Mike Jacobs, who Wirtz felt was *"losing his hold on boxing."* The Chicago Stadium owner suggested that a mutually protective agreement be put in place for their buildings. Wirtz closed by saying that this solution might be the only way to resolve the situation. This letter solidified the government's case that Norris and Wirtz had conspired to create a monopolistic empire.

The government also discovered other damaging documents from the general's extensive business correspondence library that showed that Norris and Wirtz had communicated with Madison Square Garden representation prior to the formation of the New York and Illinois boxing clubs. These companies would eventually become the instruments in the men's restraint-of-trade practices. After nine days of testimony, the federal hearing came to a close.

The IBC's counsel, Whitney Seymour, asked Judge Ryan to dismiss the case, which he rejected.

JUDGE RYAN: "I am going to reserve decision on your motion to dismiss. I feel a very serious question of law is presented here. I feel that very factual issues, if any, are presented. I think this case might almost be tried upon a stipulated set of facts. Perhaps there may be some dispute as to the inferences to be drawn from the facts which are undisputed and whether or not these inferences find sufficient support in the evidence, but I don't find many factual issues here."

The International Boxing Clubs would now await their fate, but the hounds were closing in, and the distant barking was coming closer with each passing day.

26. *(Left to right):* Carmen Basilio, Norm Rothschild, and Johnny Saxton. *Courtesy of Ada Rothschild.*

11.

Taking Care of Business

sugar Ray Robinson, entering his fourth match against Bobo Olsen, was out to prove that it wasn't a *"lucky punch"* that took down the tough Hawaiian-born fighter in December 1955. The three previous contests had been lopsided in Sugar Ray's favor, and he wanted to finish off Bobo once and for all. It was time to move on to someone else. He was not looking past Olsen and prepared for a hard fight. This was not the time to have a bad performance. He would box Olsen, content to wait for the challenger to make a mistake, and then he would let him have it. He was mentally and physically prepared to fight fifteen rounds.

Bobo Olsen, after being knocked out early in the last match, had indicated that his goal was very simple: he needed to fight smarter. He must make the older Robinson fight into the later rounds, where he perceived he would begin to dominant the match. Bobo recognized that he had to fight inside because he lacked the speed, power, and skills to box Robinson over fifteen rounds from a distance. His strategy was to physically wear down his older opponent by mauling him in clinches, keeping the pressure on at all times. If he could do this without getting careless, he could win the title back.

●　　●　　●

LOS ANGELES, MAY 18, 1956. A crowd of 20,803 filled Los Angeles's Wrigley Field, setting a new California record for boxing receipts, grossing $228,500. The challenger fought smartly through the first three rounds, careful not to get into a slugfest with the more powerful champion. Olsen bullied his way in close, his hands high, elbows in, smothering Robinson's punches. He applied consistent pressure, trying to wear the champion down. In the fourth round, Olsen got careless, leaving himself open. Robinson smacked him with a solid right to the body, followed by a left hook to the jaw, dropping Bobo to the canvas. The explosive impact of the two lightning-quick punches turned Olsen's legs to jelly, and he collapsed to the canvas. When referee Mushy Callahan's count reached seven, Bobo weakly tried to get to one knee but fell back as Callahan counted him out. The time was 2:51 of the fourth round.

In winning the fight, Sugar Ray Robinson had scored his 90th knockout in 145 professional bouts. His convincing win over a good opponent confirmed he was back at the skill level to battle the best middleweights. The big gate plus another $100,000 for television fees had given Robinson and Olsen a huge payday. Unfortunately for Bobo and Sugar Ray, their two six-figure checks were never cashed by either of them. Olsen's share was attached to his estranged wife Dolores's divorce action. Robinson's was gobbled up by the IRS for unpaid back taxes.

SUGAR RAY ROBINSON (Boxer): "I didn't get a chance to test my legs because the fight didn't go long enough. Bobo hit me hard in the third round, but that was his ruination. After that punch he gained confidence and began coming in. I hit him flush on the jaw. I wasn't sure I had him until the count reached ten."

BOBO OLSEN (Boxer): "I guess he's got a jinx on me. I'm better than what I showed the last couple of fights, but make no mistake that Robinson is a great fighter."

•　　•　　•

Carmen Basilio was so frustrated over his loss to Johnny Saxton in Chicago that he decided to go to New York and ask the New York State Athletic Commission for its help. He pleaded with the commission to let Saxton sign his own contract: "New York is the only place I can get a fair shot. Please allow him to fight in New York."

Commission chairman Julius Helfand was on record stating that people like Blinky Palermo were no longer welcome in New York boxing. He was adamant about not ever giving Saxton's manager a license in New York State. Basilio's emotional appeal had not totally caught him by surprise. He admired Basilio for his honesty and character but had concerns about making allowances for Saxton to fight in New York. He would be going against what he had been advocating, keeping people such as Palermo out of New York. This was no time to backtrack.

A meeting with James Norris convinced Helfand to rethink his position regarding Saxton. Norris told the commissioner that for the "good of boxing" he should allow this match to happen in New York. The furor over Saxton winning in Chicago had the public incensed over the shabby way Basilio had been treated. Norris assured him he had nothing to do with the questionable decision, but his organization was being unfairly criticized for what had happened. If a wrong had been indeed committed, then Helfand could right that wrong by allowing Saxton to sign to fight in New York. Helfand saw the logic of Norris's appeal and told Jim to let him sleep on it. He wanted some time to look at all the possible scenarios before making a decision. A frustrated Helfand pointed out to the IBC president that boxing was being kicked around because only a handful of its top executives had stood fast to clean up the sport. He respected Norris for siding with him against the Managers' Guild, saying that more crusaders needed to come forward and be united in this battle: "Boxers like Basilio need to feel that they can get a fair shake wherever they fight." James Norris, sitting directly across from Helfand, nodded his head in agreement. Walking Norris to the door, Helfand reiterated that he would be in contact soon regarding his decision. What James Norris didn't know was that Helfand had already decided to allow Saxton to sign a contract to fight Basilio. The commissioner would make his most improbable ally wait twenty-four hours before telling him. Julius Helfand felt good about allowing this fight to happen in New York, but there was one major flaw in his thought process: By sanctioning this fight, he was benefiting a guy he was trying to run out of boxing. He was benefiting Frankie Carbo.

Syracuse boxing promoter Norm Rothschild had put Syracuse on the map as a good fight town. Jim Norris and Ray Arcel had both copromoted television matches with Rothschild, with Carmen Basilio being the star attraction on Arcel's Saturday Night Fights. When the bigger arenas were not available for television fights, Syracuse became the backup. Rothschild promoted fifty-six nationally televised fights from Syracuse, making it the third-largest number of boxing fights shown on television in the entire country. Only New York and Chicago showed more fights on television.

Born and raised in Syracuse, Rothschild got his first taste of boxing while selling programs in the 1930s at fights at the old Syracuse Arena. In 1948, he purchased the Salina Diner across the street from the Syracuse Arena, renaming it Norm's Arena Restaurant. Dubbed the "boy promoter" by writer Red Smith, the young, energetic Rothschild was always friendly and outgoing. He would talk boxing with everyone he came in contact with. Rothschild's Arena Boxing Club presentations were always first class, staged at the Onondaga County War Memorial. Built in 1951, the War Memorial was a modern facility in the mid-1950s, which could hold up to nine thousand fans for boxing.

ADA ROTHSCHILD (Wife): "A guy by the name of Eddie Gallagher and Norm got together and borrowed Henny Andrews's license. There were two local fighters in Syracuse that people talked a lot about, and they thought if they got together, people would come out to watch them fight. Unfortunately, the commission wouldn't approve the fight. So they promoted another fight, but it wasn't the same, and he lost money on that deal. He then decided to get his license and have Eddie Gallagher make the matches. The next fight was the Joey DeJohn and [Robert] Villemain, and that fight sold out in about two hours. We had a phone booth in the restaurant, and that phone kept ringing off the hook. Next door was Ray Stortel's Liquor Store, and I would write the phone orders down and send the whole page next door to Ray to put the tickets up. That was a huge success. That began him becoming a fight promoter."

Norm Rothschild had been in contact with Gabe Genovese about the second Saxton-Basilio fight. Rothschild desperately wanted to promote the fight in Syracuse. Genovese told Rothschild that if the fight came off, Norm probably had little chance of getting it. Genovese said that he thought Norris and Carbo were planning the fight for New York. Genovese agreed with Rothschild that the fight would generate a nice gate in Syracuse. Rothschild asked Genovese what could be done to get the fight moved to Syracuse. Genovese said that Carbo owed him a favor, but it would "cost" Norm to get the fight moved to Syracuse. "How much?" Rothschild asked Genovese. "It'll cost you ten thousand dollars."

Rothschild told Genovese that he thought ten thousand was a bit extravagant, but he would see what he could do. His next call was to James Norris, who told him if he could work it out, he could have the fight. Rothschild called Genovese back and said he had a deal. A week later Johnny Saxton signed a contract to defend his title against Carmen Basilio in Syracuse. The Arena Boxing Club would copromote the fight with the International Boxing Club of New York. Genovese and Carbo each made an extra five thousand dollars.

DONNIE HAMILTON (Boxing Historian): "Norm Rothschild was one of the most honorable men I ever met. A good guy. A good-hearted guy. He loved Syracuse, and he loved boxing. He had no choice but to work with those guys. Otherwise, this area would not have had those great fights."

Carmen Basilio went right into training. He pushed himself harder than John DeJohn wanted but couldn't control. Basilio had taken the defeat by Saxton hard, much harder than he would let on to the media. This fight was his "career fight." A loss would push him so far down the welterweight ladder that it could be years before he got another title shot. He'd be out of the game by then.

The confidence that he had displayed going into the first fight with Saxton was still there, but it had been channeled more into an anger toward the champion, for whom he had little respect. He had achieved his championship by outlasting a guy who had laid it on the line against him. Tony DeMarco fought him until he had nothing left to give. Basilio identified with that. If he was going to lose his title, he wanted it to be like DeMarco lost his: going down fighting, knowing you had given it your all, and your all just wasn't quite good enough. He could live with that. There was no shame in that. But losing it the way he had was wrong. He couldn't allow a fighter like Saxton to be welterweight champion. He didn't deserve it, and he sure as hell hadn't earned it. The next time . . . damn his jab . . . damn the referee . . . he would destroy Johnny Saxton. It was the right thing to do.

● ● ●

SYRACUSE, NEW YORK, SEPTEMBER 12, 1956. The reigning welterweight champion, Johnny Saxton, was greeted with a chorus of boos as he entered the arena to face Carmen Basilio. The Onondaga County War Memorial crowd of 8,596 in full voice screamed a constant stream of obscenities at Saxton as he went through his prefight routine. When his opponent, Carmen Basilio, climbed into the ring, the crowd stood and cheered his every movement. Basilio, attired in white satin trunks with black trimming, had weighed in at 146¼ pounds, a half pound more than the champion. Basilio, a 6-5 favorite, glared at Saxton while listening to referee Al Beryl give instructions. Saxton stared back with no expression, still surprised by the anger the crowd had toward him. He expected a partisan crowd but was taken back by the degree of negative emotion directed at him. It was far worse than he had expected.

Carmen Basilio went right after Johnny Saxton at the beginning of the bout, but instead of retreating, the challenger held his ground. Saxton met Basilio at center ring and slugged it out with him through the first two rounds. Saxton the boxer, "the hit-and-run" specialist, was not fighting that way tonight. He was out to show the boxing public, especially this rude crowd, that he could beat Basilio at his own game, in his own backyard. An aroused Saxton, fed up with hearing he was given the title in Chicago, was going to prove right here, in the middle of the ring, that he was the better man. He hit Basilio with combination after combination, smacking him in the face and midsection, forcing Carmen to cover up from the speed and accuracy of his punches. His nostrils flaring, the pent-up anger pouring out of him, Saxton hit Basilio hard and often. Basilio, bobbing and weaving, kept coming, moving forward, taking three punches to get one, refusing to back away from the punishment. His face a crimson red from the steady barrage of jabs, he refused to retreat. Basilio was putting it all on the line. There were no other options—he had to win.

In the third round Basilio began to find his range, physically punishing Saxton with vicious hooks to the body. By the middle of the fourth round the champion began to backpedal, changing his tactics in an effort to move out of range of Basilio's relentless attack. With a welt under his right eye, Basilio returned the favor in the fifth, raising a welt under Saxton's eye, scoring a hard right that was set up by a left hook to the body. In the seventh, Basilio split Saxton's lip open with a solid right hand, a wound that would later require nine stitches to close. Basilio stayed in control through the eighth round as Saxton began to visibly tire. A confident Basilio told his cornerman Angelo Dundee that the end was near. "I'm going to knock him out, Angelo. It's coming soon."

"Good. Let's get out of here. You don't get paid extra for going fifteen rounds," Dundee replied.

"See you soon," Basilio shouted back as he charged out for the ninth round.

A minute into the round, Basilio caught Saxton with a left hook that dazed the champion, forcing him backward. Basilio stalked him, blasting a hard right to his jaw that wobbled his knees. With Saxton now defenseless, Basilio pushed him against the ropes, where he rained punch after punch on him, knocking

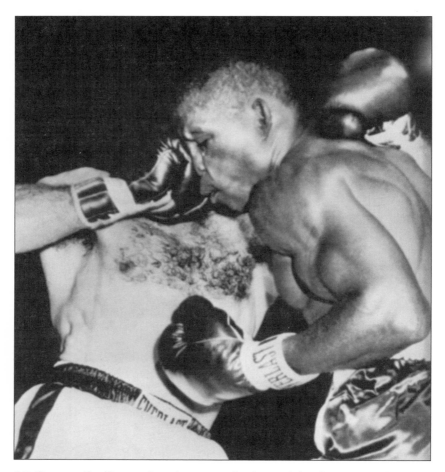

27. Carmen Basilio mashes the nose of welterweight champion Johnny Saxton. *Courtesy of AP Images.*

him senseless. Referee Al Beryl moved in to stop the carnage as Saxton began to tumble to the canvas. Acting quickly, the referee grabbed the wounded fighter and helped him back to his corner. Carmen Basilio had regained his title in one of his most inspiring performances. In his mind he had righted a wrong. He wept openly in the ring, overcome with the emotion of completing his mission. The fight had been stopped at 1:31 in the ninth round. The welterweight crown was back in good hands. James D. Norris, sitting ringside, smiled.

28. Carmen Basilio collapses into the arms of Joe Nitro and Johnny DeJohn after winning the welterweight championship. *Courtesy of AP Images.*

Prior to the fight, a cocky Blinky Palermo had told the press, "You fellas keep saying that my boy won the title with the help of the officials who robbed Basilio. Well, tonight he's going to prove to everybody that he's the master. He'll fight Basilio's style and beat him at his own game. He'll prove he's the better man." Following the fight, Palermo took a different tack, saying it was the referee's fault his guy lost. "He did a bad job. He never should have stopped the fight in the ninth until Johnny had hit the deck at least once." Then, strangely, he told the press the exact opposite of what he had said prior to the fight.

BLINKY PALERMO: "I don't want to criticize Whitey Bimstein, for I think he did a fine job in the corner with that cut, but if it had been me in the corner I wouldn't have allowed Johnny to fight with that bad tear. Carmen fought a good fight but I can't understand why my boy changed his style."

Palermo went on to say that it was a great fight and that there would be a return bout when "WE are ready."

When Saxton would be ready to fight again was anybody's guess. The veteran cornerman Whitey Bimstein said the cut on Johnny's lip was the worst he had seen in more than thirty years in the business and thousands of fights. It would be days before Saxton would find relief from the pain. A heartbroken Saxton, sobbing uncontrollably in his dressing room following the fight, was affected by the reception from the biased Syracuse fans.

JOHNNY SAXTON: "I don't know why people don't like me. I try hard. I have no excuses . . . he just beat me . . . but the people here just don't like me. You have no idea how tough it is to go to someone else's hometown. Encouragement is the greatest thing in the world and I didn't have any tonight. I tried to fight his type of fight for the first five rounds, then when I went into my style for a minute they start booing me so bad I changed again. I want a return bout anywhere but here. The people here don't deserve the next bout. They saw a good fight tonight."

ARTHUR DALEY (Writer): "If a fighter's combative style is that of a rabbit, he's only asking for trouble when he pretends that he is a tiger. Saxton asked for such trouble in Syracuse Wednesday night, when he fought Carmen Basilio whose proud boast is 'I'm the toughest guy in boxing.'"

Promoter Norm Rothschild's investment to make the fight happen in Syracuse had been well spent, as the fight produced a record gate of $134,951. Saxton took home 40 percent, which with television fees amounted to a touch over $75,000. Basilio received 20 percent for his efforts, which ended up at $37,662. The new welterweight champion said he was through fighting for the remainder of 1956. He and his wife, Kay, were heading up to the Thousand Islands and a well-deserved vacation. He would let manager John DeJohn figure out the next fight. When asked how he would do against Sugar Ray Robinson, Basilio gave a confident reply: "If I fight him, I'd lick him. I'd weigh 150 to 151 for the bout." John DeJohn the following day told the press, "We are not interested in Robinson. He will have to adjust his mathematics to make a fight with Basilio happen."

29. Basilio Training Camp, Alexandria Bay, New York. *(Left to right):* Joey Basilio, Joe Nitro, Archie Whitfield, Carmen Basilio, Leo Owens, two unidentified men, and John DeJohn. *Courtesy of Carmen Basilio.*

12.

Training Camps and Boxing Gyms

throughout his career Carmen Basilio concentrated on becoming a better boxer through hard work and enormous determination. He enjoyed the rigors of training and the preparation of a big fight. Training was as much a part of his life as eating, drinking, or breathing. He embraced the discipline and the pride that come from the extra hard work that would pay dividends later on in a tough match.

CARMEN BASILIO: "I'm always happy when I sign for a fight. I know that I'm going to go into training. I like to train. It means that I'm gonna get away from the banquet circuit and I get a little bit of peace when I am in training. The phone doesn't ring and I can relax."

KAY BASILIO (First Wife): "Every time Carmen is booked for a fight he is overjoyed. He tells people he's only in the boxing for the money. I know it's really in his heart."

During training he was up at five thirty, running four miles, alternating sprinting and jogging. Each day he would focus on increasing the sprinting portion of the four-mile run. Back at camp, breakfast followed, which consisted of orange juice, three soft-boiled eggs, toast, and coffee. The closer he got to the fight he would cut out the coffee, substituting tea in its place. After breakfast he would catch a quick nap, followed by his daily routine of exercise designed to increase his stamina and strength . . . then it was on to sparring. Many days, Basilio would run out of sparring mates, and John DeJohn would have to literally push him out

30. Training taken at Sylvan Beach, New York. *(Left to right):* Joey DeJohn and Carmen Basilio. *Courtesy of Don Hamilton.*

of the ring. His love of sparring never changed throughout his career. He would finish the gym portion of his training by shadowboxing. Carmen would stand in front of a mirror perfecting his moves, always working at increasing his speed. Once the workout was done, Joe Nitro would give him a rubdown, then it was off to fish the rest of the day.

He would withdraw from people during camp, only occasionally playing cards or "shooting the bull." He preferred to fish or take long walks. It was his way of getting himself mentally prepared for a fight. At night, he would eat a large meal consisting of meat, plenty of vegetables, and salad. Following the evening meal, Carmen liked to watch films of fighters, making mental notes to himself about their styles and imagining how he would fight them. As the training progressed, he added additional work in the gym and had less free time for fishing. Relentlessly, he pushed himself into prime condition.

JOHN DeJOHN: "Outside the ring, Carmen never has changed, but not so during training. He had a more carefree attitude in his early career with us but there was a gradual change as he moved up the ladder and smelled the big money. Carmen became motivated by a driving desire to reach the top. In training, he withdrew to himself, got more edgy and needed the solace of bowling, hunting or fishing to take the edge off. In more recent fights he has gotten real mean in the days immediately preceding a bout. On one occasion he got real short with his wife Kay during the morning of a fight. She understood, but it bothered Carmen that Kay might have been hurt. In the dressing room he said, 'Hey Johnny, go find Kay and tell her I'm sorry.'"

GREG SORRENTINO (Boxer): "Carmen taught me to get up early and do roadwork. He stressed that it takes discipline to do it. You must get up early and do your four miles of roadwork, because when everybody else is sleeping, you are out there working, paying the price. Run a half a mile, then sprint a hundred yards, run backwards a hundred yards, shadowbox . . . run another half mile, running in boots, then doing the same thing over and over each day. We used to do sit-ups and toe touches, I mean hundreds of them. I thought I was in shape when I started to work with him, coming off a year of college football. He put me on this training regime, and I thought he was crazy."

When Carmen was between fights he stayed in shape by working out at the Main Street Gym in Syracuse, often referred to as the Robbins Gym, located on the third floor in the 300 block of North Salina Street. It was a typical boxing gym, loaded with boxers, trainers, promoters, writers, and fans. Similar to most boxing gyms in the 1950s, the emphasis was never on cleanliness, as if dirt and grit and foul odors made boxers train better. It had one ring, a couple of heavy bags, and a speed bag. The best area fighters worked out at the Robbins Gym, besides all the out-of-town boxers who were in town for a fight. Main-event fighters were charged fifteen dollars per month, whereas preliminary fighters were charged ten dollars per month. Amateur fighters could work out for four dollars a month. If you wanted a towel, it would cost you ten cents. Irv Robbins always complained that he was forever chasing, looking for people who owed him money.

CARMEN BASILIO: "He knew how to run a gym. He wouldn't stand for any fooling around, or he would throw you out on your ear. He wouldn't take any shit from anybody. It was a good place to get your work done. He knew his business."

DONNIE HAMILTON (Boxing Historian): "Irv Robbins knew boxing. He knew the fighters and how to get ahold of fighters. He was a character himself. I always referred to Irv as the Damon Runyon of Syracuse boxing. I never have met a guy like him in my life. Prior to a boxing show in Syracuse, Rochester, or Buffalo he took care of the undercard. Norm Rothschild went by him. He knew the fighters, he knew the matches, and he knew how to put fighters together, and he knew how to get fighters wins. He'd bring in the right guy; there was no business done. He would bring in a guy who he thought could lick a guy. Also, if he wanted to get you licked, he could do that to. Irv would yell at people, curse you out like nobody's business. Today they would lynch him. He couldn't get away today the way he talked to people back then. I remember one day this fighter came in from out of town for a fight, and Irv yelled at him. Up to then I never heard a fighter talk back to Irv. This guy yells back at Irv, 'Don't talk to me like that, old man. You're not talking to those other people. You had better be careful what you say to me.' I thought, my God, what's this guy doing? That would be like yelling at the pope. Irv never said a word. He just walked out of the dressing room. Well, this guy leaves, and Irv says, 'I'm going to take good care of that guy.' He has a fight coming up, and Irv gets him an opponent. He finds some kid that had three pro fights in Philadelphia, but had something like nine hundred amateur fights. He had been in the ring a lot and knew what he was doing. He almost killed this guy. Irv got even. That's the way he was. He could get you knocked off. He could get you a win, or he could get you licked."

When Carmen Basilio would fight in New York he would go to Stillman's Gym for a workout. The great *New York Post* columnist Jimmy Cannon referred to Stillman's as the post office of the fight game. Promoters who were looking to fill their fight cards would call the phone booths at Stillman's to talk with the managers about what fighters were available. All the top fighters of the day trained at Stillman's, right next to the wannabes and never-weres who dreamed of becoming champions. Sugar Ray Robinson, Rocky Marciano, Willie Pep, Archie Moore, Rocky Graziano, Floyd Patterson, and Carmen Basilio all worked out there. Dreams were created and destroyed at Lou Stillman's joint. That was the nature of the business.

In 1919, Louis Ingber was summoned to the estate of Alpheus Geer to discuss an opportunity to become the manager of the Marshall Stillman Athletic Club. Geer and his business partner, Hiram Mallison (both wealthy New York socialites), wanted to create an athletic program that would instill pride and discipline in some of the city's young criminal element. Geer believed that teaching these misguided misfits the art of boxing would help lead them to an honorable lifestyle. In Ingber, a former law enforcement officer, Geer felt he had the right man for the job. Although Ingber had no experience in operating a gymnasium, he had vast experience in dealing with lawbreakers. Geer thought that this type of experience was necessary for his program to succeed. He needed a tough guy who could control these young hoodlums while instilling some discipline and pride in them. Geer and his partner, Mallison, would oversee the business aspects of running a gymnasium. Ingber was hired on the spot, and the gymnasium opened for business the next day.

The patrons, from the beginning, mistakenly referred to Ingber as Stillman. Young Lou didn't much care what they called him because he didn't particularly like any of those people anyway. If they thought that was his name on the sign outside, let the bastards think it. He was not about to tell them any different. If he actually did own the place, the first thing he would do is throw these bums out on their ear. But it wasn't his place, so he would put up with it. He would do his job.

Alpheus Geer's idea to rehabilitate these young delinquents had merit, in theory, but in practicality it missed the mark. There were continual problems with various things coming up missing, which frustrated Geer's manager, Louis Ingber. He had very little patience to begin with, and then having to deal with these ungrateful "scumbags" on a daily basis made his demeanor all the more unbearable. Geer kept encouraging Ingber "to hang in there," telling him that things would improve. They were doing good work, and programs like this would take some time before they would see some positive results. Besides, Geer was investing his own money and time trying to make the program work, not to mention attaching his good name and social position to the project. He encouraged his manager to have patience, as things would get better. Ingber needed the paycheck, so he went along with Geer, although he thought that this altruistic idea had little chance of succeeding. Very few of the criminals took the program seriously, which irked Ingber to no end. Most of the time they didn't show up, and those who did went at the training with little enthusiasm. The only real fighting that occurred was when there was an argument over a card game or someone was caught stealing.

Finally, things came to a head when the gymnasium was broken into one night and all the boxing gloves were stolen. The next day Geer informed his manager that he had seen enough; effective immediately, the Marshall Stillman Athletic Club was closing its doors. This came as no big shock to Lou Ingber, who had expected this to happen for some time. Geer's rehabilitation program was failing miserably, and it was time to shut it down. Although Ingber personally couldn't stomach the criminals he dealt with at the gym, he did recognize the need for a training facility for boxers who were serious about training. Professional boxing was becoming popular with the public, and there was some movement to legalize the sport in New York State. Each day, more and more young men were turning to the sport as a way to make a living.

There was a definite need for a gymnasium for these young men who needed a place to train.

Fighters such as Benny Leonard, Jess Willard, and the up-and-coming heavyweight contender Jack Dempsey were making headlines across the country with their fists. The elite writers of the period, Damon Runyon, Westbrook Pegler, and Grantland Rice, kept fight fans enthralled with stories about the current champions.

Lou Ingber, wanting to capitalize on the growing interest in boxing, moved quickly to secure from Geer whatever equipment that had not been stolen. Ingber was still owed some final compensation and cleverly made this part of his exit income. He discovered some available space farther uptown and within a couple weeks opened Stillman's Gym. Later, Lou Ingber legally changed his name to Lou Stillman. He would hold court over the world of boxing for the next forty years.

JIMMY CANNON (Writer): "The stooped old man spoke a private language of insult and carried a thirty-eight bulging from his hip. The voice was grouchy and harsh. If New York could talk it would sound like Lou Stillman. The great champions trained there as did the ones with the brains punched soft in their heads. It was a bleak loft with dirty windows, and you reached it by going up a dark flight of splinted wooden stairs. There were two rings and in the big days of boxing, fighters stood in line and practiced two at a time from morning until dusk. Upstairs on a balcony, were the heavy bags and the speed bags."

RAY ARCEL (Trainer and Promoter): "Grupp's Gymnasium was actually where all the great fighters trained following the First World War. Billy Grupp, who owned the gymnasium, kept getting drunk and would berate the Jews, saying they were responsible for the war, that all the German people got killed because of the Jews. Well, who happened to be training at the gymnasium at that time? Benny Leonard, Benny Valgar, Abe Goldstein, Willie Jackson, Marty Cross, Sammy Good, all of these Jewish fighters. So when they heard this one of the fellows said, 'You know, there's a new gymnasium opened up on 125th Street, near Seventh Avenue . . .

Let's go take a look at it.' We liked what we saw and began training there. Stillman knew nothing about professional boxing but he knew who Benny Leonard was. Pretty soon when word got around that Leonard was training at this new gym, you couldn't get into the place. Lou was Lord and Master of the thing. He charged fifteen cents for entry to watch some of the best fighters of the day compete. The Gym was filled with boxers, trainers, managers, and hanger-ons. It was best remembered for its smell (which writer Sam Toperoff said included every foul male odor ever made), and for Stillman himself, who treated every fighter, champion, or bum the same—badly."

A. J. LIEBLING (Writer): "Many famous people trained there but mainly boxers. Jack Dempsey, Georges Carpentier, Primo Carnera, Fred Apostoli, Joe Louis and Rocky Marciano were some of the famous world champions who trained at Stillman's Gym over the years. One who refused to train there was Gene Tunney, because he complained about the place's sanitation, saying that he would never train there unless the windows were opened. Typical of him, Stillman refused to open the windows. Boxers paid six dollars a month for a locker and eleven dollars a month for a dressing room, which means a stall just wide enough for a rubbing table. The deluxe dressing rooms had hooks on the plywood partitions. Stillman had a microphone in back of his stand and in the back of his head a rough list of the order in which fighters will go into the rings. Some fighters he knew by sight; trainers had to prompt him with names of others. He said the names into the mike and they would come out equally unintelligibly, so it didn't matter. Most of the spectators know who the guys were despite the headgear that made them look like witch doctors."

ROCKY GRAZIANO (Boxer): "Stillman's Gym don't look no better to me than I did to Stillman. Up at the end of a long, dark stairway is this barn of a place. In the middle are two regulation-size rings, with big lights over them. It's a good thing there are big lights because the windows look like they haven't been washed in years. Even the pigeons that hang around out there have given up looking in for free at the fighters. One thing I like about this joint my first day there, I see that everybody spits on the floor at Stillman's, and spitting is an old habit I got. In the ring to the left a couple of guys are slugging each other. They're wearing head gear but one of the guys is taking a beating in the face and bleeding out of his nose . . . And nobody is paying much attention to them, except a trainer who leans on the edge of the ring, looking bored and chewing on an old cigar stub. In ring number two, a half dozen guys are galloping around shadowboxing. Behind the rings, some guys in trunks are shadow boxing, others are doing pushups. From up on the balcony comes the noise of the punching bags—whappity, whappity, whappity . . . every third and fourth minute the bell rings for the rounds . . . and under the clock off to the left is Lou Stillman, who is looking more bored than anybody else, keeping track of who's in the ring, and who is due in next like a checker in a parking lot. This is the famous Stillman's Gym."

A. J. LIEBLING (Writer): "A spectator must pay twenty-five cents at a turnstile manned by a fellow called Curley, who is an expert at non-recognition. For years he has practiced looking at people he knows as if he had never seen them before. The boxers, managers, and trainers who use Stillman's naturally get in without paying admission, and they sometimes bring their friends. When this happened, an agonized look spreads over Curley's wax-like face. He resents introductions as buildups for future free entries, and makes a point of forgetting them."

Carmen Basilio admitted he never liked working out at Stillman's because it was so crowded with fighters. "They were a bunch of animals. You had to wait in line to do everything," he would say later about his experiences at Stillman's. In 1959, Stillman's Gym closed, a victim of televised boxing, and eventually it was torn down. Years later, Stillman told Al Braverman that it was the worst thing he could have ever done, as it left him with nobody to talk to.

DONNIE HAMILTON (Boxing Historian): "The only difference between Lou Stillman and Irv Robbins was that Stillman carried a gun."

31. Basilio KO's Saxton in Cleveland. *Courtesy of AP Images.*

13.

1957

gene Fullmer, part-time welder and mink farmer from West Jordan, Utah, was next up for Sugar Ray Robinson, with their championship fight scheduled for New York on January 2, 1957. The fight was originally planned for December 12 but had to be rescheduled when Robinson claimed he was sick with a virus. This twenty-fifth postponement of Robinson's career rankled Fullmer because he and his handlers would now miss Christmas at home. Robinson's sudden illness only added to Fullmer's frustrations of dealing with the problematic champion. It started when Sugar Ray had demanded an outrageous split of the purse before he would agree to the match. Fullmer was offered a paltry 12.5 percent to fight for the middleweight title. Fullmer was furious with the offer, but his father convinced him that by beating Robinson, there would be bigger paydays down the road. Fullmer grudgingly agreed, but it caused tremendous animosity leading up to the fight.

Gene Fullmer, an elder in the Church of Jesus Christ of Latter-day Saints, never fought in a saintly manner in the ring. His overly aggressive style concerned Robinson's handlers, who asked the New York State Athletic Commission to "acquaint" Fullmer with the rules of clean fighting. Robinson's people were not calling Fullmer a dirty fighter; they had concerns with Sugar Ray getting head-butted as the result of Fullmer's "charging forward" method of boxing. They did not want the champion needlessly cut about the face or eye because of the challenger's aggressive nature.

Gene Fullmer had turned pro in 1951, winning his first eleven fights by knockout, with most of his matches not lasting past the second round. His recent win over Charlie Humez, then the number-one-ranked middleweight, had catapulted him near the top of Robinson's list behind only Carmen Basilio. A confident fighter, he believed he had earned his shot at the brass ring.

GENE FULLMER: "I wouldn't want to fight Robinson if I didn't deserve it, but I think I've worked hard for the chance. I'm ready for him and I think he is ready to be taken. I know I can do it."

A great high school athlete, Fullmer had played basketball and football while also developing into one of the best cross-country runners in Utah.

GENE FULLMER: "Basketball and football were too rough for me. I lost a tooth in basketball and almost ruined my knee in football, but in boxing I've never been hurt. A few minor bruises that's all."

Sugar Ray Robinson's first title defense since knocking out Bobo Olsen the previous May would be a tough physical test for the champion. He arrived in New York two days before the fight, deciding to spar a couple of rounds to show the public he was ready to go. In the first round he clobbered his sparring mate, Lee Williams, with a series of combinations that staggered the Harlem middleweight. Following his impressive two rounds of sparring, he entertained everyone as he hit the light and heavy bags for one round each, pounding both bags with his impeccable timing and rhythm. He declared, following the workout, that he was mentally and physically fit for the upcoming fight. There would be no excuses from him if he didn't successfully defend his crown.

●　　●　　●

NEW YORK, JANUARY 2, 1957. New York fight fans turned out in huge numbers to witness the Robinson-Fullmer battle at Madison Square Garden. An announced crowd of 18,134, the highest attendance in years for boxing, witnessed an aging champion attempt in vain to hold back the advances of a swarming Gene Fullmer and Father Time.

The challenger, from the opening bell, attacked the champion inside, scoring to the body with pistonlike precision, easily winning the first three rounds. In the sixth round, Fullmer rocked Robinson with a solid left to the chest, which sent him sprawling backward into the ropes. Fullmer then maneuvered inside where the two fighters clutched so tightly that they tripped, knocking the lower strand of the ring post down. In the seventh round Fullmer hit Robinson with a solid right-left combination that knocked him through the ropes. Sugar Ray, up and back in the ring as referee Rudy Goldstein's count reached six, traded long-range bombs with Fullmer the remainder of the round. The fight remained a war throughout the match, with Sugar Ray hitting Fullmer with punches that had floored Bobo Olsen but only ricocheted off the challenger's head with little damage. Robinson, bleeding from his left eye, his white trunks stained with blood, entered the last round needing a knockout to win. He attacked Fullmer furiously, pounding his opponent with solid left and rights, but the young fighter refused to back away and kept boring inside, dishing out his own form of punishment. The Garden crowd, in complete bedlam, drowned out the final bell as the two warriors fought past their allotted time.

Sugar Ray Robinson had survived fifteen rounds of physical pounding and was still standing when it was all over. This paradoxical man, who had run out on so many fights, broken so many hearts, had once again rallied the New York faithful with his tremendous courage and determination. Many people who didn't care for the person he was outside the ring had to give him his due inside the ropes. He never ran out on a fight inside the ring. In that fifteenth round, he had used his complete arsenal of punches. He jabbed, he hooked, he hit Fullmer with uppercuts, but he couldn't knock him down. He appeared to be a shadow of what he once was. Perhaps this great champion had reached the end of the road. Fullmer had clearly won the fight on all cards inside and outside of the ring.

SUGAR RAY ROBINSON (Boxer): "There is nothing I can say but the better man won tonight. I certainly wasn't as sharp in my punching as in other days. I never have missed so many punches in my life, but you must not forget that this fellow Fullmer is tough. I hit him good enough to finish him several times. But he blinked his eyes and just kept coming. I don't know whether age has anything to do with my showing tonight. I felt good most of the way. The only point about the difference in ages tonight might have been that when you are younger you can take it better."

The new middleweight champion of the world had his mother and father sitting ringside, sharing this special moment with him. His father, Lawrence, known as "Toughie" back home for his impatient demeanor, was standing . . . cheering his son's victory.

LAWRENCE "TOUGHIE" FULLMER: "I knew he could do it. He always did have what it takes. He's been a fine youngster and a fine, religious man. He was in beautiful condition. He took the best Robinson had and let him have it right back. He's my boy! I did box twice some years ago, but mostly it was street fighting. That's quite a different art. The rules are different."

MRS. FULLMER (Mother): "I just couldn't look at those boys all the time. This boxing is men's business and I don't care much for it. But our boys always have liked violent exercise and they seem to thrive on it. Who am I to say no?"

Gene Fullmer showed up early the next day at the International Boxing Club's office to pick up his share of the purse. Fullmer received $20,915.60. The deposed champion received $138,190.11 for his share. The fight, blacked out in New York, had generated the largest gate revenue at Madison Square Garden in years. The lobby was jammed prior to the matches, with many people having to be turned away. It seemed like old times again with the huge crowds descending on the Garden to watch a fight. Televised boxing matches were having a negative effect on "live boxing" across the country. No longer could the small venues afford to stay in business, as people preferred sitting at home to watch boxing three nights a week on television. The ripple effect of this new trend was felt by many boxers and trainers across the country, their opportunities to box becoming fewer and fewer.

James Norris met with Gene Fullmer and his manager, Marv Jensen, to discuss a return bout in May 1957, either in New York or in Chicago. Norris told Fullmer that the fight could possibly draw a gate of $250,000. The young champion's eyes lit up over that huge potential payday. His father had been right after all. The next time around he would be paid 30 percent for his services. He would be an equal partner.

Sugar Ray Robinson sent his representative, Ernie Braca, over to the IBC offices to get his money. Braca also met with Norris, who outlined what he had discussed with Fullmer and his thoughts about a return bout, assuming Robinson was interested. Braca assured Norris that Robinson was interested and that Sugar Ray would be in touch in a few days to fine-tune the proposed contract. James Norris grimaced at the thought of what lay ahead to get this lucrative bout arranged.

GENE FULLMER: "Peanuts . . . I fought for expenses this time, but the next time I'll be out for the big money, and I'll keep the title, too. I'll be twice as mean and I'll try for a knockout. I wanted to do that last night, but Jensen [his manager] told me that I had the fight won, so I didn't take any unnecessary chances."

MARTIN KANE (Writer): "So passes the brightly lighted Robinson era. It ended in the 15th round, when the plodding tortoise beat the flashy hare once again, as he always does in the fable. Sugar Ray Robinson had thought he was living another kind of fable, which is what the hare always thinks."

•   •   •

Holding on to the welterweight belt the past few years had been a very difficult proposition for the reigning champion. Since Kid Gavalin had surrendered the title to Johnny Saxton in Philadelphia, on October 29, 1954, there had been three champions, with only Carmen Basilio able to successfully defend his title.

Saxton, in his first title defense, was knocked out by Tony DeMarco, who then was TKO'd by Basilio. Basilio put an end to that trend by stopping DeMarco in Boston in November 1955, but Saxton took the crown back by winning in Chicago, before losing it back to Basilio in Syracuse. The crown now back in Basilio's possession, could Carmen successfully defend it? And was he physically ready to do so?

Carmen Basilio set his training camp up in Miami, at Angelo Dundee's Fifth Street Gym, away from the snow and cold of central New York. The condition of Basilio's right hand continued to be the main topic of conversation leading up to the third battle with Johnny Saxton, this time in Cleveland, Ohio. The fight had originally been scheduled for January 18 but was pushed back to February 22 to allow the champion's sore hand to heal. It had never been right since he hurt it in the second DeMarco fight, and this caused some concern with how healthy Basilio would be for his second title defense.

JOHN DEJOHN: "There is nothing wrong with Carmen's right hand. If there was, we wouldn't have him fighting. Yes it's a little sore, but Carmen's a tough guy and can deal with the pain."

This "rubber match" between the two fighters would be the first championship fight in Cleveland since Sugar Ray Robinson knocked out Jimmy Doyle in June 1947. Sadly, Doyle later died of injuries suffered during that fight. Robinson, so distraught over Doyle's death, recounted later that he had dreamed the night before the fight that this tragedy might occur; it only added to his distaste for being a professional prizefighter.

Johnny Saxton, determined to win back the welterweight title, stated that he was in the best shape of his career and would outbox Basilio this time. He would not foolishly slug it out with him at center ring like he did in Syracuse. Saxton told the press that he would revert to his jab-and-run style that had won him the welterweight title in Chicago. This type of fighting would stymie Basilio's desire to fight inside, which would allow Saxton to maintain better control of the fight.

●　　●　　●

CLEVELAND, FEBRUARY 22, 1957. A disappointing crowd of 8,514 turned out to watch this third and final installment of Basilio-Saxton. The champion entered the fight a 12-5 favorite, down from the 3-1 odds he was a week prior to the fight. The condition of his right hand still cast some doubt over his chances to defeat Johnny Saxton. Carmen Basilio, again dressed in white satin trunks with black trim, entered the ring to a standing ovation. Johnny Saxton, similar to his entrance five months before in Syracuse, was booed by the Cleveland fans, who let him know they were here to see him box, not run. He again remained expressionless throughout the prefight introductions.

The first round saw Basilio aggressively attacking Saxton with a series of punches that were vengeful and purposeful. He rocked Saxton with a left hook a minute into the fight as he relentlessly punished him with a series of stinging combinations to his ribs and jaw. Basilio ignored Saxton's futile jabs, forcing himself inside, where he blasted away. Saxton barely survived the first round, wobbling back to his corner. In the second round Basilio moved in, intent on ending the fight early. He battered Saxton around the ring, belting him with solid left-right combinations. The challenger, groggy, his eyes glazed, gallantly fought on before a vicious left hook found its mark and he dropped to the canvas. As referee Tony LaBranche's count reached ten, Saxton struggled to his feet, but it was too late; mercifully, he had been counted out. The Cleveland Arena erupted in cheers for Carmen Basilio, who had put on another sensational performance. He had decisively defended his title with an impressive knockout. The injured right hand that had pushed the fight back five weeks was not a factor. The champion had used it just enough to set up his left hook, which ended the fight.

Carmen Basilio now had finally finished his business with Johnny Saxton. The memory of Chicago and his bitter defeat there was washed away in the euphoria of a tremendous victory. The time had come for this little man from the onion fields of Canastota. His last two fights against Saxton and his thrilling two knockouts of Tony DeMarco made him arguably the hottest box-office fighter in the game. There were no welterweights on the scene to fight that excited boxing fans or him. It was time to look upward toward the middleweight division. A championship bout outdoors at either the Polo Grounds or Yankee Stadium against the winner of the upcoming Gene Fullmer rematch with Sugar Ray Robinson would draw huge numbers. IBC president James Norris made it clear following Basilio's stunning performance in Cleveland that he was on deck, with a middleweight title fight taking place probably in New York in late summer.

For Johnny Saxton, his time as a championship contender was coming to an end. He would retire a year later, finishing his career with a 55-9-2 record. He would leave the game with little money and many questions about a checkered career that might have turned out better if the boys in the back room had not controlled him. He deserved better.

CARMEN BASILIO: "I knew I had him in the first round when I hit him with that left hook. Those head shots were all right, but those punches to the body, that's what took it out of him. I certainly hit that fellow with a lot of leather."

NAT FLEISCHER (Editor, *Ring Magazine*): "A throwback to the days when champions were truly fighting men, Carmen Basilio, the former onion farmer, cut loose with a two-fisted attack that put an end to the aspirations of Johnny Saxton to regain the crown he had lost to Carmen. The fans love a hard-hitting champion and they have one in Carmen Basilio."

The following day the champion held court with the media at the Hotel Statler in downtown Cleveland. He was sitting on top of the world. He talked openly and honestly about his future in boxing: "Look, as long as I can win and make money I will keep on fighting. The strain is beginning to tell . . . especially on my family. My wife takes these fights harder than I do. When there's no money and the fights are tougher, it will be time to get out. I would like to fight the winner of the upcoming Robinson/Fullmer next summer, because I don't believe there are any welterweights out there that I can't lick."

CHARLEY GOLDMAN (Rocky Marciano's Trainer): "If a fellow is a delicate fellow and has no punch, he's going to be clever.

He's got to be exceptionally clever . . . but Basilio was never delicate and he could punch, so that's why he is what he is."

When Gene Fullmer returned home to Utah, he submitted his resignation as an apprentice welder at the Kennecott Copper Company. The new middleweight champion would be a bit busy over the next few months.

GENE FULLMER: "Welding has always been something for me to fall back on later if necessary. I have been holding that job to keep my family going. What little I earn as a boxer I put in the bank for the future. I didn't make a fortune in that first fight, though it represents more than I have ever made in the ring and much more than my annual salary as a welder. I have made a number of contracts contingent upon my winning the title and those contracts will take up so much time that I couldn't very well ask my employers for an unlimited leave of absence. So I am submitting my resignation."

The Utah strong boy with a seventeen-inch neck approached the first defense of his title with quiet confidence. Always in superb condition, Fullmer was ready to apply the same tactics he had used in his first fight with Robinson: always moving forward and always punching. He believed that he was too strong for Sugar Ray. His aggressive style of fighting would again be too much for the aging challenger, who would tire in the later rounds. Robinson's punches did little damage to him in the first fight, and he was not afraid to take a few to get inside. Besides, he had a score to settle on the putrid amount of money he had received the first time around. He wouldn't be fighting for "peanuts" this time. Fuller was to receive 30 percent of the gate, which was expected to be around $150,000, and 30 percent of the television fees. There was much at stake for Gene Fullmer when he entered the ring on May 2, 1957. His mother and father and his wife would again be ringside to root him on.

Sugar Ray Robinson once again was faced with a must-win situation, with the majority of fight scribes across the country believing his career was over. Boxing was a young man's game, and the thirty-seven-year-old former champion had stayed too long. He should have known better after what happened to his close friend Joe Louis, when he had stayed too long in boxing. Robinson didn't believe that he was through as a fighter and trained hard for the rematch, focusing on his timing and fundamentals. The greatest technician in the history of the sport had missed badly with his punches in his first encounter with Fullmer; he understood that would have to change if he was going to have a chance to regain the crown. No opponent had ever beaten him twice in his career, and he was not about to let it happen with Fullmer. Pride was a big factor in his motivation, but the need for money, as always, was his means to an end.

*   *   *

CHICAGO, MAY 1, 1957. A horde of writers greeted the two fighters as they appeared for their noon weigh-in. Sugar Ray arrived last, surrounded by his posse of trainers, managers, family, and friends. Walking up to Fullmer, he stuck out his hand to the reigning champion. "Hello, Gene, how do you feel?" The pair shook hands, with the surprised Fullmer just nodding back at Robinson.

Gene Fullmer entered the Chicago Stadium a 9-5 favorite to defeat Sugar Ray Robinson. The powerful twenty-five-year-old champion, with a record of 40-3, twenty by knockout, was primed to wage a countersurge attack on Sugar Ray Robinson's body. The challenger came into the return match a pound under the allotted 160-pound limit with his own ideas on how this fight would be fought. It would be a completely different fight this time.

The opening stanza began with Fullmer again providing most of the action. The challenger was content to be passive, holding the young champion, preventing him from getting inside. Late in the first round Robinson whacked Fullmer with a couple of left hooks to the head that appeared to do little or no damage. Sugar Ray continued the same approach through the second three minutes, probing his opponent, looking for weaknesses but allowing Fullmer to easily win the round. Robinson's methods suggested that he was waiting for Fullmer to make a mistake. He may not be winning the early rounds, but he hadn't lost the battle. He was executing his plan.

In the third round, Fullmer became frustrated with the pace of the fight and began taking more chances, trying to get inside. He wanted Robinson to lead, which would allow him to counterpunch while bullying his way in close. Robinson cleverly stayed back, not forcing the action, making Fullmer *create* the action. The champion took the bait and moved in, throwing punches from all angles but with little effect. In the fourth round Robinson started fast, hitting Fullmer with two rights as the champion bored in unconcerned, slapping left and rights to Sugar Ray's body. This time, Robinson, instead of grabbing and holding, traded blows with Fullmer, clearly getting the best of the exchange and finally winning his first round of the fight.

Gene Fullmer came out for the fifth round determined to take back control of the fight. He aggressively attacked Robinson, belting him with a series of punches to the body. Robinson again grabbed and held Fullmer, forcing referee Frank Sikora to break the two fighters apart. A frustrated Fullmer drew boos from the crowd as he punched Sugar Ray on the break. Slowly, Robinson was discovering a pattern to Fullmer's fighting; each time he would snap off a punch, Fullmer would lunge forward. Robinson began peppering him with a series of jabs from both hands, inviting him to come inside. Sugar Ray feigned a left, hitting Fullmer with two solid rights to the body, which surprised him, pushing him to his right. Sugar Ray instinctively stepped back, then delivered a short left hook to the jaw of Gene Fullmer, who never saw it coming and slumped to the canvas. Rolling onto his back, the champion was out cold. His reign of 177 days as middleweight champion was over. In an instant, like a lightning bolt from the sky, he was knocked unconscious.

Ray Robinson had again validated to the world that his career was not over . . . he wasn't ready for a rocking chair just yet. In regaining the middleweight championship for the fourth time, he had reaffirmed his lofty position as one of the greatest "one-punch" fighters in ring history. He could set his opponent up for the big punch by maneuvering him into position. Olsen and Fullmer had the styles to beat him, but both got sucked in by his wizardry and ultimately paid the price.

Later, in his dressing room, a bewildered Gene Fullmer asked his manager why the referee had stopped the fight so quickly. Marv Jensen informed him that he had been counted out. Fullmer, besides not seeing the devastating punch that knocked him out, was unaware of how he had struggled to get to his feet. Now despondent on the news of his being knocked out, he told his manager, "I'm sorry, Marv. I know I let you down." Jensen, wrapping his arms around his fighter, who was like a son to him, softly replied, "It's okay, Gene, I'm just glad you're not hurt."

GENE FULLMER: "That's the first time I got knocked out and I don't know how it happened. He's the greatest fighter I have ever met. He's got the best record and he's the only one that ever knocked me out."

MARV JENSEN: "I think Gene wanted to make a spectacular fight because he was champion and it cost him his championship. We warned him in the corner to fight like he had before . . . keep his hands up and crowd. But he didn't do it."

SUGAR RAY ROBINSON (Boxer): "I was just maneuvering him trying to draw him in with a right. That right was a decoy. I wanted a clean counter shot with my left. I finally got it. I don't know how far the punch traveled but I'm sure Mr. Fullmer got the message. I just thank God I got that punch in, because I had no other strategy."

Sugar Ray was very humble following the fight, going out of his way to thank his fans and his good friend Joe Louis, who he said had kept faith in him when others had turned their backs. He also singled out his wife, Edna Mae, who, he said, "had suffered untold miseries as I prepared for this fight."

Sugar Ray basked in the satisfaction of winning back the middleweight title in such dramatic fashion, pleasantly answering all questions. Behind him, three Internal Revenue Service men stood near a shower stall, politely allowing him to enjoy his moment in the sun. They were there to collect the government's slice of his pie. Earlier, a tax lien of $23,000 was put on Robinson's share of the purse. The mismanagement of his various businesses by people who took advantage of him led to his seemingly unending tax problems. Sugar Ray's businesses included a bar, three dry cleaners, a café, and part-interest in a barber shop.

ERNIE BRACA (Robinson Comanager): "If you want to be nasty about it, there was stealing going on. It took several forms. A bartender in Sugar's café, for one, had taken the job for something like one hundred and twenty-five dollars a week, and parlayed that into a pretty good deal. The day he was asked to leave, he did it gracefully, stepping from behind the mahogany, out the door, into a brand-new Cadillac. Several people were missing when we began to overhaul the situation. A quarter of a million was gone. The people didn't do it in a way which was noticeable at first . . . they simply took in the money from the various operations, gave Robinson his share and withheld the government's tax share. Somehow the government never received the money."

BLANCHE HOLLY (Robinson's Aunt): "Mr. Robinson was very young when he started these businesses in Harlem in 1945. He had confidence in his hired help and managers, but they lacked the qualities to run businesses properly. When Mr. Robinson returned from Europe in 1954, he found his businesses in appalling shape. In 1955, members of his family and experienced managers took over."

Each man received a total of $67,479 for his efforts. This included the share of both the gate receipts and the television fees. The paid attendance was 14,757, with a gross gate of $158,643. When Robinson was asked the next day by a fan what he had done in this fight that he hadn't done in the first fight, Sugar Ray simply said, "I won."

James Norris, prior to leaving Chicago for the Kentucky Derby, told the press that a fight between Sugar Ray Robinson and Carmen Basilio could do $750,000 in Yankee Stadium. Norris said he was going to try to schedule the fight as soon as he could. Later, Sugar Ray concurred that he was in favor of a fight with the welterweight champion. Basilio, who watched the fight from ringside, said he wanted a crack at Robinson and felt confident that he would do well against him. Even former champion Gene Fullmer thought a Basilio-Robinson match made the most sense. Basilio's handlers knew getting both names on a contract to fight was going to be a problem because of Robinson's penchant for wanting a bigger split of the purse. DeJohn made it clear that his guy would get an equal share or there would be no dream fight.

JOHN DEJOHN: "Basilio is just as good a gate attraction as Robinson. Don't forget, my kid is the welterweight champion. We have offers out there besides fighting him. If he thinks we're going to fight for 'peanuts,' he has another thing coming. We want the fight, but on even terms. If not we will move on."

GEORGE GAINFORD (Robinson Trainer): "Basilio will have to remember that Ray is the middleweight champion of the world, that he is in the driver's seat and that the fans come to see him. Any deal with Basilio must be made with that in mind."

A match between these two champions made for a dream fight: two proud men who hated to lose. Their competitive natures and styles of fighting guaranteed fight fans a classic battle between the supreme boxer and a hard-nosed battler. James Norris, more than anyone else, understood that getting both to sign on the dotted line would also be a classic battle.

NAT LOUBERT (Writer): "The match plays up all the 'if's,' 'and's' and 'but's.' 'Robinson is too old and Basilio will soften him up around the belly,' some insist. 'Robinson has the canny ring craft plus the ability to put a man away with one punch,' point out his adherents. Ring tradition has it that a good chin and solid left hook are the best assets any fighter can possess. Robbie and Basilio have both."

Sugar Ray Robinson, a few days following his exciting knockout of Gene Fullmer, declared that the proposed championship fight with Basilio would be his last. "I'll defend the title against Carmen

Basilio, if the terms are right. If I win that's my last fight, if I lose then of course I will try to get it back."

Robinson said the fight would take place in New York, in September, for tax reasons and because he didn't want the summer heat to be a factor. The Joey Maxim bout in 1952 had taken such a toll on his body that he never wanted to take the slightest chance of that happening again. Basilio said he preferred a bout outdoors in July or early August. Joe Glaser, Robinson's manager, said that Robinson was looking for 35 percent of the receipts. In Syracuse, DeJohn immediately responded, saying the Basilio camp would accept only a 30-30 split. While James Norris and his IBC staff went about trying to get the fight scheduled, Basilio went cross country to fight a series of exhibitions in Oregon and California. He remained confident throughout the tour that the IBC would convince Sugar Ray that there was so much money on the table that he would agree to an even split. Thirty percent of a potential gate of $1 million was far better than 35 percent of nothing. Sugar Ray was a businessman; he would see the logic in it. Basilio learned quickly that Robinson viewed the fight from a different perspective.

SUGAR RAY ROBINSON (Boxer): "This fella has had very few paydays during his life time. Let's face it . . . I'm the fella' that's making the gate. Don't I have a right inasmuch as I'm signing away my services, to get all that they are worth to me?"

CARMEN BASILIO: "He has this attitude that he's going in to Yankee Stadium alone . . . and he is drawing the crowd. . . . It takes two to make a fight. I feel I'm justified in getting as much as possible."

Promoter Norm Rothschild, anxious to have Basilio fight at least one championship bout in Syracuse, sent the Basilio team a telegram in Oregon while they were on the exhibition tour out west, saying, "Gentlemen: Will top any offer you have received for Carmen Basilio to defend his welterweight title. Ready at the date to be selected by you. Terms 40% of all monies with privilege of guarantee. Confident more money available here for defense with any leading contender."

John DeJohn wasn't against his fighter taking a welterweight championship match in Syracuse, but the Robinson fight in New York, at Yankee Stadium, would generate numbers that Rothschild could only dream of. If Robinson refused to budge on his share of the purse, the fallback position was to accept Rothschild's offer, probably against Gaspar Ortega in July. For now, that decision would have to wait to allow James Norris more time to put the middleweight title fight together.

In the preceding days, George Gainford stayed on the offensive, telling the press that if Basilio wanted a crack at the title, he would have to accept 17.5 percent of the gate. "The International Boxing Club tells me Basilio wants twenty-five percent. He'll never get it. We won't fight him for that. If Basilio loses its only one fight to him. He still has his title. But, if he wins he's got the middleweight title. As for Robinson he's got nothing to gain but a gate and every thing to lose." Gainford went on to reason that Basilio was similar to Sugar Ray when he had fought Jake La Motta, back in 1951. Robinson, like Basilio was now, had been the welterweight champion trying to move up. "Ray accepted seventeen and a half percent of the gate when he fought La Motta for the crown. Now don't go telling me that Basilio is any more of an illustrious welterweight champion than Robinson was; if anything, it's the other way around." Gainford then added that Basilio had better make up his mind pretty quickly, because otherwise they would look around for someone else to fight.

Sugar Ray's manager also divulged that they were keeping an eye on the upcoming fight between Gene Fullmer and Tiger Jones. "If Jones wins, it would be the perfect match. Jones beat Ray on a ten-round decision in 1955. It would be an ideal chance for Ray to avenge the loss and we would set up the fight for Yankee Stadium in September. If Fullmer wins then we would look to fight the Frenchman, Charlie Humez. There's no demand for another Fullmer fight, so that would definitely be out at this time." Gainford then officially threw the gauntlet down about who was calling the shots regarding the fight: "If Basilio doesn't like what we're offering and decides to take another fight before fighting Ray, that will be all right with us; but his percentage will go down to fifteen percent. We are going to call the shots."

The day following George Gainford's ultimatum, Carmen Basilio knocked out Harold "Babyface" Jones in the fourth round in Portland. Some writers expressed pity for Jones, who happened to be the whipping boy for Basilio's irritation over Gainford's remarks. Regardless of the motivation, Basilio was contrite about the Robinson camp's position: "I will let John work out the details, but I am not fighting him for 17 percent of the gate. If that's the position they are going to take . . . there will be no fight."

James Norris, besides his typical battles with Robinson over a contract, was also catching flak from him over reports that movies of his sensational knockout of Gene Fullmer were being shown in South America. Robinson claimed that there was an agreement in place that prevented any filming of that fight being shown without his permission. Norris countered by saying if there was any movie revenues collected, then Sugar Ray would receive his percentage. In addition to his problems with the middleweight champion, the IBC president was on the outs with Floyd Patterson's manager, Cus D'Amato. Patterson had won the heavyweight title on November 30, 1956, knocking out Archie Moore. The two had been chosen to fight for the crown when Rocky Marciano retired. D'Amato did not like the IBC and their relationship with the Mob. Now that he represented the heavyweight title holder, he threatened to bypass the IBC on all championship fights. He began talks with Emil Lence, a New York promoter who owned the East Parkway Arena. Lence had offered Patterson a "$175,000 guarantee" to defend his title at the Polo Grounds. D'Amato was no longer returning phone calls from James Norris.

In early June 1957, the IBC announced that Carmen Basilio had signed an exclusive contract with them to fight Sugar Ray Robinson. Basilio agreed to accept 25 percent of all receipts, which could balloon his share to more than $1 million. Basilio said he realized that he had to give a little to make this fight happen but would give up no more of his share. An angry Robinson, following a meeting with Norris, lashed out at the IBC, saying he was through working with them: "Norris knows what percentage I'll want when we get this picture business straightened out. I told him two weeks ago that I wouldn't take less than forty-five percent, no matter what Basilio got. I won't do any more business with the IBC until they pay me for my picture, even if Carmen Basilio is signed to fight me."

Robinson was cleverly divulging a host of problems he had with the IBC, which would provide some bargaining chips when it came to finalizing the Basilio fight. This tactic was designed to weaken the IBC's position. Robinson understood that for each concession he would eventually give, it would increase the overall profitability of his Basilio contract. He was setting James Norris up just the way he had set up Fullmer and Olsen: he was maneuvering him into position for the big hit. A puzzled James Norris said that Robinson was the only party that had contacted him about movies of the Fullmer fight being shown in South America: "I told Ray we've never heard from anybody but Robinson, that the pictures were being shown anywhere. I told him to hire the best law firm in New York and check the theaters that showed them and then sue them. I told him that we would pay the cost of everything. What more can we do?"

Emil Lence, observing the problems that the IBC was having with Robinson, now turned his attention to the middleweight division. He offered Sugar Ray a staggering 47.5 percent of the gate receipts if he would sign with him. Lence was now pressing to become a major rival to the IBC; he was providing the perfect third-party foil for Robinson. Sugar Ray announced a few days later that he was jumping from the IBC to Lence. The walls were cracking all around the IBC. There was blood in the water, and the sharks were circling.

The days of James Norris and the IBC controlling championship boxing matches were dwindling. They had been found guilty the previous March of violating the Sherman Anti-Trust Act by monopolizing the conduct of title fights. Federal judge Sylvester J.

Ryan had recently begun hearings to listen to opening arguments on the penalties to be included in his final judgment against James Norris, Arthur Wirtz, their two IBC corporations, as well as the Madison Square Garden Corporation.

William J. Elkins, chief attorney for the Department of Justice, wanted a dissolution of the Norris-Wirtz promotional association with Madison Square Garden representations. He also asked for a separation of the ownership and operation of arenas by Norris and Wirtz from the promotion of championship fights. Last, Elkins wanted the pair to be forced to sell their joint stock interest in Madison Square Garden Corporation. Norris and Wirtz's legal counsel, Kenneth Royal, called the proposed selling of the Garden stock "excessive" and appealed to Judge Ryan to allow his clients the option of selling their stock in the Madison Square Garden Corporation or getting out of boxing completely.

JUDGE RYAN: "Quite frankly speaking, I don't look with favor upon any decree compelling Norris and Wirtz to throw their stock upon the open market, because not only they might be penalized, but it is also possible that others not involved in this case would suffer substantial losses."

William Elkins then amended his position regarding the stock, stating that six months would be a more reasonable time for the two defendants to sell off their stock. If the stock was not dispersed within that time frame, then it would be placed with a court-appointed trustee to be disposed of "promptly at a fair and reasonable price." The trustee would have "the sole right and duty" to vote the stock pending its sale. Judge Ryan, the next day, said he had reached a tentative conclusion that the duo of James Norris and Arthur Wirtz must be broken up.

JUDGE RYAN: "The great evil I found was the combination that Norris and Wirtz caused and created by joining up with Madison Square Garden. I regard Wirtz and Norris as one, and the Madison Square Garden as another separate entity and business interest. The evil primarily sprung from their combination, their concerted efforts and actions. That has to be broken up. The IBC's are nothing more than corporations reflecting Norris and Wirtz. They serve no purpose except to distribute the profits of Norris and Wirtz. I am heading to a decision that I am reluctant to take, that both IBC's be dissolved. If they want to give up their outside interests, they can continue their interests in the Garden."

Truman Gibson, secretary of both the New York and the Illinois IBCs, testified that the two corporations had only two fighters under personal service contracts: Carmen Basilio, the welterweight champion, and Sugar Ray Robinson, the middleweight champion. Gibson pointed out that in years past, the two corporations had exclusive contracts in most weight classes.

On June 24, 1957, federal judge Sylvester J. Ryan ordered James D. Norris and Arthur M. Wirtz to sever all connections with Madison Square Garden Corporation. He also ordered them to dissolve the International Boxing Club of New York and the International Boxing Club of Illinois. They were given five years to dispose of their stock in Madison Square Garden Corporation. Within thirty days of the final decree, Norris and Wirtz had to resign as officers of Madison Square Garden Corporation. They were still permitted to operate as a Chicago Stadium group. Judge Ryan's goal was to once again create healthy competition for championship fights. He pointed out that since 1953, Norris-Wirtz interests had promoted twenty-four out of thirty-seven championship fights presented in the United States. The Garden would be allowed to promote two championship fights per year but none with the assistance of James Norris or Arthur Wirtz. Both Madison Square Garden and the Chicago Stadium should be made available to other promoters on a "reasonable rental basis."

The following day, James Norris finally received a bit of good news when Joe Nitro phoned him, stating that Carmen Basilio was staying with the IBC. He would honor the contract that he had signed with the IBC in early June. John DeJohn and Joe Nitro were receiving offers daily for Carmen Basilio to fight in a number of cities. Besides Norm Rothschild's interest in him fighting in Syracuse, they had offers from St. Paul, Newark, and Philadelphia. Promoter

Nick Troilo guaranteed Basilio $75,000 to fight Joey Giardello in the Quaker City in August. None of these offers was taken seriously by the Basilio camp, but they provided options and their own form of a bargaining chip. DeJohn understood where Gainford and Robinson were coming from, but he also knew that his guy was a key part to the puzzle, regardless of what they said. Everybody knew Robinson needed money, and Basilio at 35 or 40 percent was still the best "money fight" for him. Eventually, they would have to come around to them.

The IBC was offering 40 percent to Robinson, but he was demanding 45 percent. The 5 percent had to be made up somewhere. Norris met with Basilio prior to his meeting with Sugar Ray Robinson. Basilio informed Norris that he was going to defend his welterweight title against Gaspar Ortega if Norris couldn't get Robinson to sign soon. Everyone involved understood that they needed each other, regardless of what was portrayed to the media. This was the fight that America would pay to see. Robinson wasn't getting any younger, and Norris's days in boxing were numbered. Also, Basilio had never had a potential payday like this would provide . . . it was time to get together. Three days later, it was announced that Sugar Ray Robinson had agreed to terms with the IBC to fight Carmen Basilio in New York City in September 1957. The exact time and date and where the fight would be held were not disclosed. Robinson would receive 45 percent of the gate, with Carmen Basilio receiving 20 percent. James Norris said in regards to Judge Ryan's recent decree that he believed it didn't apply to this fight, because negotiations had begun prior to the hearings. A return-bout clause was also included in the contract, with a 30-30 split if Basilio was to defeat Robinson. The fight would take place within ninety days. Also in the news that day was that Floyd Patterson's manager, Cus D'Amato, had agreed to Emil Lence's offer, and his fighter would defend his title at the Polo Grounds on July 29 against Tommy "Hurricane" Jackson.

The Sugar Ray Robinson–Carmen Basilio middleweight title fight was scheduled for Yankee Stadium on Monday, September

23, 1957. Robinson, in his fourth reign as middleweight champion, again set his training up at Greenwood Lake, New York. Robinson said he expected to come in at his customary 159 pounds, one less than the middleweight limit. Carmen Basilio hoped to enter the fight at 153, 7½ pounds above his normal fighting weight. If he was able to defeat Robinson at that weight, he would have the distinction of being the lightest middleweight champion in ring history. Moving up in weight class didn't concern Carmen Basilio or his handlers.

JOE NITRO (Trainer): "Those middleweights, they may be bigger but they can't get into the condition Carmen can. The other day mind you, we're up in Syracuse and Carmen comes into the gym . . . he spends an hour and a half punching the big bag, the speed bag and that was after he walked fifteen miles, shooting for partridge up in Madison county. Nobody's going to hurt a fellow in that type of condition very badly."

Ray Robinson continued to pressure James Norris on every financial aspect regarding the fight, now questioning the IBC's choice of what company should present the pay-TV bout. Norris had assigned the rights to Theater Network Television, a company that the IBC had used for the Rocky Marciano–Archie Moore fight in 1956. The telecast had grossed $282,000, and it was expected that the number would increase. There would be approximately 375,000 seats available for the bout, representing some 151 theaters. Sugar Ray argued that TelePrompTer, Inc., would be a better choice to handle the telecast. Robinson threatened to pull out of the fight if Norris didn't switch to TelePrompTer. Later, Sugar Ray backed off his demands but was given a larger number of tickets for his dispersal. Sugar Ray leveraged every aspect of the fight to his financial benefit. He saw the IBC problems as his opportunity to increase his share of the purse.

One morning while James Norris was working in the IBC offices finalizing some details of the upcoming fight, he began to complain of chest pains and was rushed to the hospital. The immense strain from all the pressure he had been under recently had caught up with him, and he suffered a heart attack. He would spend the next seven weeks in the hospital recuperating. All IBC business would now be conducted from his hospital room. People of all walks of life came to see him, with one fellow in a gray suit quietly appearing in the late afternoon at least twice a week.

On July 29, 1957, Floyd Patterson TKO'd Tommy "Hurricane" Jackson in the ninth round before a sparse turnout of 14,458 at the Polo Grounds. This heavyweight championship fight had generated only $156,936 in gate receipts. Cus D'Amato waived the "$175,000 guarantee" that Floyd Patterson was supposed to receive in favor of a 40 percent return. This kind gesture saved Emil Lence from taking a financial bath. Patterson and D'Amato still made out financially on the bout, but old Cus won the respect of boxing promoters for his generous concession. Later, he said if it had been the IBC he was dealing with, he wouldn't have forfeited a dime.

Carmen Basilio set his training camp at Alexandria Bay, in the heart of the Thousand Islands region of upstate New York. Basilio enjoyed training in this picturesque setting because of the friendliness of the townspeople, who made him feel right at home. It also allowed him to go fishing when he wasn't training.

CARMEN BASILIO: "It was the perfect spot for me to train because I could get my work in and then fish, which is something I love to do. Plus, the people there were so friendly to just not me, but everyone connected with my training. It was great."

When the New York State Athletic Commission sent Dr. Charles Heck up to Alexandria Bay to give Carmen Basilio his prefight physical, he was amazed at what he found.

DR. CHARLES HECK: "I have examined intercollegiate champions in track, crew, football as well as amateur and professional boxing. I can honestly say that this young man is in the finest physical condition possible. I have never seen an athlete in the condition this boy is. He's remarkable."

Following Dr. Heck's physical, the welterweight champion of the world demonstrated to the doctor why he was in such good shape, putting himself through a grueling two-hour workout that included five rounds of sparring with two different fighters. In the first session, he pounded sparring partner Archie Whitfield for three rounds, with solid punches to the head and body. Afterward, the tall middleweight from Chicago remarked that he was "glad he wasn't fighting him." Basilio used fourteen-ounce gloves during his sparring to protect his oft-injured hands. In the second sparring session, Basilio went two rounds with his longtime sparring mate, Leo Owens, also pounding him with vicious combinations to the body. In the second round Basilio hurt Owens with a left hook and had him against the ropes as the bell sounded, ending the sparring session.

Sugar Ray Robinson worked out five days a week, taking Sundays and Thursdays off in preparation for his fight with Carmen Basilio. Each workday he would rise at six and run six miles before returning to his mountaintop cottage, which he referred to as his "cabin in the sky." After breakfast, he would rest until three o'clock, when he would do his gym work. One day his sparring might emphasize the jab; another day he might work on sharpening his hook or focus on defense. When he completed his sparring he would hit the heavy bag and the speed bag, ending his two-hour workout with an entertaining rope-skipping exhibition. He treated the fans who spent $1.10 to attend his training sessions with nonstop entertainment.

In preparation for what he hoped would be his last fight, Sugar Ray seemed to be at peace with himself and his good fortune to have regained the middleweight title. He took an intrinsic pride in his negotiation skills, hammering out what he wanted and standing up for what he believed was right. Yes, he was getting paid much more than his opponent, but in his mind he was worth every penny. No matter what Basilio and his people said, this was a big fight because *he* was involved in it. He was sorry about James Norris being hospitalized and the way some writers portrayed him in the papers—he wished those people knew him better, knew that there was more to him than what was publicly displayed.

SUGAR RAY ROBINSON (Boxer): "I've made mistakes . . . many of them. But I try to do the right thing and hope that I can always do it. What may be right with me, may be wrong to others. I want to be nice to people. I want people to like me. Who doesn't? But I can't be everywhere at the same time. I'm a human being, just like everyone else. I have a right to some privacy and a right to my opinion. I'm a businessman and boxing is my business. I have the right to drive the best bargain I can for myself as any other businessman. I have been crucified in the press for many things I have done. That is their right. I hold no ill feelings for that although a good deal was unjust. Right now, I want to finish my boxing career in victory, God-willing, and continue to live happily with my family."

This complex champion was, as Jimmy Cannon portrayed him, a study in contradictions. He brokered a better deal than anyone in the fight game but applied little acumen to his business empire. He was an extremely religious man, yet he chose to practice only those aspects of religion that fitted his lifestyle. He loved children but rarely spent time with his own. He appeared greedy to most people in boxing, yet for a dollar he fought Charlie Fusari in 1950 and donated the rest of his purse to the Damon Runyon Cancer Fund. Sugar Ray Robinson was many different people to many different people—no one ever knew for sure which one would appear.

In the days leading up to the fight various opinions were provided on who had the upper hand in a match between a welterweight champion and a middleweight champion. Most observers had the same impression about this fight that they had with Robinson's two previous fights against Fullmer: If it went fifteen rounds, Basilio would win because the aging champion would tire in the later rounds. If the fight was stopped, it was because Robinson had knocked Basilio out. How Robinson would fight a smaller man was also discussed. Sugar Ray, even when he was a lightweight, fought almost exclusively with welterweights. Then when he moved up to the welterweight division, he fought mostly middleweights. He even fought light heavyweight champion Joey Maxim, soundly beating him before the heat got to him. Would fighting a shorter and lighter fighter cause him problems? He was clearly the better boxer of the two, but Basilio was a rugged fighter, similar in style to Fullmer and Tiger Jones, both of whom had defeated Robinson. Robinson had always had trouble with fighters who crowded him, and Basilio was a master at crowding. Sugar Ray had advantages in height, weight, reach, and speed of hands. Basilio was younger and as tough as they came, with an iron jaw and a desire that bordered on obsessive. He had never been knocked out. Tony DeMarco staggered him but couldn't put him down. Pro-Robinson people pointed out that DeMarco was no Sugar Ray Robinson. Basilio may have been hit hard by a tough welterweight, but he had not yet been tagged by a tough middleweight, and there was none tougher than Sugar Ray Robinson. So many angles, so many suppositions, but it boiled down to who wanted it the most. Inside the ropes these strong-willed men would meet.

•   •   •

NEW YORK, SEPTEMBER 23, 1957. Sugar Ray Robinson carried a 6½ advantage into his championship fight against Carmen Basilio, tipping the scales at 160 pounds. Basilio, in his first middleweight title skirmish, weighed in at 153½, the heaviest of his career. Basilio entered a 6-5 favorite to defeat the champion, but the odds had dropped slightly in the past twenty-four hours, as many people aligned their money with Sugar Ray. An early-morning rain had given way to partly cloudy skies with cool temperatures as the two fighters entered the ring. Sugar Ray Robinson was dressed in white satin trunks with black trim, while Carmen Basilio was attired in black trunks with the customary white trim. Basilio entered first and remained in constant motion, pacing back and forth near his corner, both fists pumping like two pistons firing in an overworked engine. Sugar Ray Robinson, climbing through the ropes a few minutes later, appeared more reserved, bouncing up and down, expressionless, clearly focused on the task at hand. Neither fighter looked at the other, each surrounded by

32. Carmen Basilio and Sugar Ray battling at Yankee Stadium. *Courtesy of Carmen Basilio.*

his cornermen. Following announcer Johnnie Addie's introductions and referee Al Beryl's prefight instructions, the robes were removed, the cornermen exited the ring, the houselights went down, and the two men stood alone staring at each other. All the talk . . . all the bad feelings . . . all the hard work . . . it didn't matter now. It was now about the two of them. Nobody else. It was time to fight.

Sugar Ray Robinson opened quickly, scoring with a series of jabs to his opponent's face. Basilio tried to counter, but his punch was picked off by Robinson, who proceeded to hit the challenger with three more jabs upstairs. Basilio, still pressing the action, finally scored with a grazing right to Robinson's jaw, who came back with a left to the body and two more jabs to the challenger's nose, causing a trickle of blood to appear. The champion's jab remained effective throughout the round, but the challenger didn't back away.

He kept coming forward, his craggy face turning bright red from the jabs, but he just kept coming. Robinson continued to score with combinations as the bell rang, ending round 1.

In the second round, Robinson again started fast, hitting Basilio with two quick jabs to the face before Basilio hooked a left to the body, followed by a hard right to the jaw; another hard hook to Robinson's ribs hurt the champion, forcing him to back up. Robinson continued to slide to his right, his jab peppering Basilio's face as he tried to set up his big right hand. The resilient challenger pressed him, ducking in close, where he blasted Robinson with hard blows to the body. The two fighters traded punches back and forth the remainder of the round. Sugar Ray had demonstrated through two tough rounds that he had the better boxing skills, but Basilio had shown his tremendous grit and determination. Something had to give. Robinson was pounding him, but Basilio wouldn't go away . . . he just kept coming back for more.

Through the first six rounds in this intense battle Robinson held a slight edge, but he was expending an enormous amount of energy. Beginning in the seventh round Robinson's punches began to miss the mark. The taller fighter was finding it difficult to hit his shorter opponent, who began to crouch, creating an even smaller target to hit. Robinson kept trying to leverage his punches, but he lost his timing. Basilio, now on the attack, forced Robinson to backpedal, now using his jab as a defensive tactic versus being the lead punch in his offensive game plan. Basilio, disdainful of Robinson's left, zeroed in on his body, slamming it with lethal left and rights, as the thirty-seven-year-old champion retreated away from the action.

Reaching the eleventh round, Robinson went back on the attack, hurting Basilio with blistering left-right combinations, smashing his young adversary with heavy body blows that rocked him back on his heels. Joe Louis, sitting next to Robinson's wife, Edna Mae, sensed his friend's physical resurgence . . . that magical moment late in a fight when energy and desire align for one last time. The "Brown Bomber" jumped out of his seat, enjoining his close friend to attack. Sugar Ray, on cue, moved inside, where the two

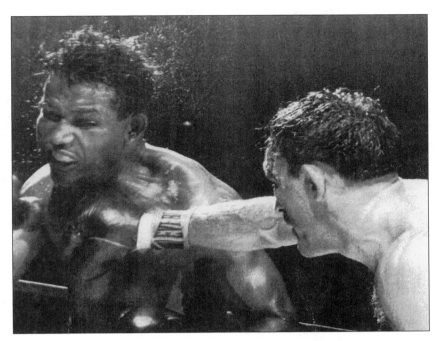

33. Basilio slams a right to Robinson's jaw. *Courtesy of Carmen Basilio.*

fighters savagely traded punches, throwing leather from all angles. Basilio, blood flowing from his nose and left eye, and Robinson, blood streaming from his nose, appeared to want to settle it right here, right now. Toe-to-toe, their eyes locked for an instant, each man oblivious to everything but the man standing in front of him. Robinson buried a slashing right hand into Basilio's midsection, followed by a vicious uppercut to the jaw; his energy soaring, he appeared to be on the verge of a knockout. He moved forward, but the challenger fought back. Basilio walloped Robinson with a tremendous shot that knocked him backward as the delirious Yankee Stadium crowd rose en masse to salute his efforts. Fighting on instinct, he battled valiantly, pummeling Robinson with punch after punch until the bell rang to end the round, with each fighter being helped back to his corner. The fight that had teetered back and forth with each round now took on a special aura. These two remarkable athletes, both exhausted and bleeding, each refusing to give in, were taking this fight to a different level. Basilio had rallied back to win the round, but the savagery of the punches, the brutality of each fighter's intent, made the previous three minutes unforgettable. Each was willing to sacrifice everything in his quest of victory—losing was not an option. They had just fought three of the greatest minutes in ring history. It didn't matter.

Sugar Ray Robinson kept up the attack in the twelfth as he again hurt Basilio with a long right to the jaw, staggering the welterweight champion and forcing him to retreat against the ropes. Sugar Ray closed in, slapping Basilio with two left hooks, but somehow Carmen stayed on his feet. Basilio finished the round by throwing wild left and rights at the champion's head . . . but missing badly. Basilio wobbled back to his corner.

When the fight moved to the fourteenth round, Robinson slowly moved out to center ring, the thirty-seven-year-old champion ducking away from a Basilio right and countering with a weak left to the body. The challenger, his face a bloody mess, moved inside, hitting Robinson with a hook to the jaw, before catching a right to his own jaw. These two boxers, fighting on guts and guts alone, fiercely battled on even terms the remainder of the fourteenth round. They closed the fight in the fifteenth round just the way they had started it: whaling away at each other. When it was over, the two fighters retreated to their respective corners, each believing that he had won the fight.

Yankee Stadium, so alive through forty-five minutes of intense fighting, became strangely silent, as everyone waited for the results to be tabulated. Basilio, in his corner, paced back and forth, his head down, silently praying to himself. Robinson, in his corner, kept moving back and forth like a caged tiger waiting to be fed—he had been through fifteen rounds of hell. He hoped he would never have to do this again. He awaited the decision. Johnnie Addie succinctly told the tale: "Judge Artie Aidala scores it nine to five and one even . . . Basilio. Referee . . . referee Al Beryl scores it nine to six . . . Robinson. The other judge, Bill Recht, scores it eight to six and one even . . . the new middleweight champion of the world, Carmen Basilio . . . Basilio."

Announcer Don Dunphy left his radio partner, Winn Elliott, and made his way to center ring, where he caught up with the new champion seconds after the decision was announced. "Congratulations, Carmen. Tell our NBC radio audience, how do you feel?"

"Thanks, Don, I'm a little tired . . . it was a tough fight. I thought I was a little out of form, but I thought I won the fight because I pushed all the way. I made the fight . . . I pressed the guy."

"I know you made it, but were you badly hurt at the end of the twelfth and thirteenth? You seemed like you might go down."

"No, he hit me with a good punch, but I was off-balance, and it made it look like I was going to go, but I was never hurt that bad that I was going to go down."

"Carmen, Robinson seemed to have the better of the early rounds. What do you think the turning point was?"

"Well, after the sixth round I started to get smart . . . I started to get down. I was standing up too straight."

"Well, Carmen, good luck."

Dunphy looked next to interview Sugar Ray Robinson, but the deposed champion had exited the ring visibly upset over the decision. The winner and new middleweight champion of the world, tears running down his cheeks, got down on his knees left of center ring and prayed.

WINN ELLIOTT (Broadcaster): "You can't take your hat off too high to the basic determination of Carmen Basilio . . . a man, shall we say, is a throwback to the caveman. I don't mean that in a disparaging sense; there's a boy, when he gets into the ring, he's in there to win. Outside the ring he's just as lovely a guy that you would ever lay eyes on. He's sweet and simple and gentle . . . he loves kids. I'm not going to get maudlin about it, but there was never a more 'Jekyll and Hyde' character than that same Carmen Basilio. In the ring a killer . . . tonight, he met a man thirty-seven years old who was supposed to be all through, if the fight went beyond seven rounds . . . he certainly wasn't. Ray Robinson still had the great punch,

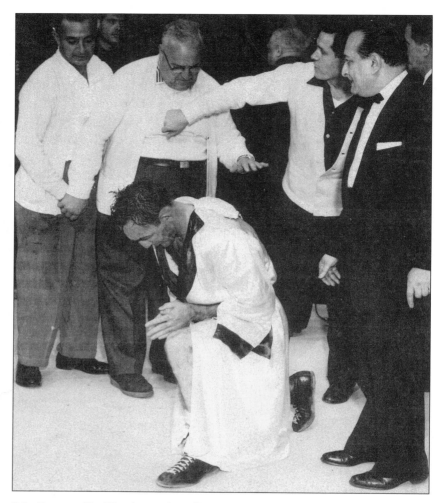

34. Carmen Basilio shown kneeling in prayer after a fight.
Courtesy of Carmen Basilio.

but it couldn't deck the solid jaw of Basilio . . . he couldn't put him down, and Carmen in all humility now is back in the center of the ring thanking his maker. He is giving thanks for the strength and the courage he found here tonight, to reach the very pinnacle of his career. A dream of this little boy who used to be an onion farmer in upstate New York, and if my voice chokes a little it's because, having met the fellow personally and his entire family, I know what a great guy he is outside the ring. Of course, tonight, he proved to better than forty thousand here what a true champion inside the ring he is too. He was battered considerably in the latter part of the fight, but only taking a breath, as it were, he came back flinging everything he had. In the opinion of Artie Aidala, who scored it for him 9-5-1, and Bill Recht, who gave it for him 8-6-1, he was the welterweight as well as the middleweight champion of the world . . . new in the latter sense. Referee Al Beryl had it 9-6 in Robbie's favor, and I can't let this microphone go Don [Dunphy] without saluting Ray Robinson, who fought a gallant fight. He was everything everybody ever said he was . . . wonderful classic fighter, knows all the tricks. Maybe the thirty-seven years were just too much."

The bout was a financial success. A live audience of 38,072 paid $556,467. The pay-TV grossed $305,000.

JOE NITRO (Trainer): "He's real smart, Carmen is. They don't credit him for that. Remember in the fight he was up straight getting hit with the jab. He went down low and got hit with a couple of bolos. Then he went into a medium crouch. Did you ever see Robinson miss as many punches as he did in there with Carmen?"

CARMEN BASILIO: "Those big fellows get so much leverage that they can hurt you, but you've got to let them hurt you. I fought Robinson. There's the best of them. He hurt me, sure, but I found a way to beat him."

JOE NITRO (Trainer): "Many times in the late rounds, Robinson bombed Carmen pretty good, but he punched right back. I think that took more out of Robinson than anything else that Carmen did in there. Robinson didn't expect him to come back the way he did to retaliate. That was Carmen's secret."

According to the *New York Times* on September 24, 1957, "The eleventh round was the single most thrilling session of the night. Basilio shook Robinson with a left to the head. Then they closed and wailed [*sic*] away at each other in a savage exchange. 'We're driving now,' Basilio said, gesturing at co-managers Joe Netro [*sic*] and Johnny DeJohn."

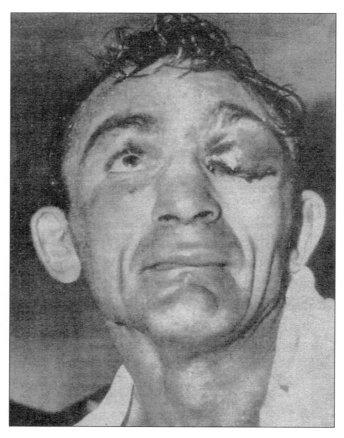

35. "The Warrior," Carmen Basilio, following the March 25, 1958, middleweight championship title bout with Sugar Ray Robinson. *Courtesy of Carmen Basilio.*

14.

1958

going back to the early 1900s, the boxing public has always had a love affair with the middleweight division, when wild man Stanley Ketchel was knocking people out by the bushelful. Unfortunately for the "Polish Prince," an irate husband caught him fooling around with the man's wife and shot him in the back. Many considered Ketchel to be one of the greatest middleweights of all time. Fearless in the ring, with little formal training in the art of boxing, he stopped forty-nine of his sixty-four opponents before a bullet stopped him at the age of twenty-four. His larger-than-life persona has grown over the years and only adds to the division's colorful history.

The middleweight division was created in 1867 when it became apparent that many very good fighters were being deprived of a chance to compete professionally because of their size. The creation of this weight class has produced some of the greatest acts of courage in pursuit of victory the sport has ever seen. These compact 160-pounders combine the power and aggression of heavyweights while possessing the speed and quickness of lightweights. The Basilio-Robinson battle at Yankee Stadium added another great saga to this popular weight class.

Carmen Basilio, on the heels of winning the middleweight title from Sugar Ray Robinson, was enjoying the adulation that comes with the championship. He had been a guest on the Ed Sullivan and Steve Allen television programs as well as interviewed by Mike Wallace and countless other topflight broadcasters. His face was on the cover of the all major sports magazines, and he was voted *Ring Magazine*'s "Fighter of the Year." He was also receiving daily business propositions.

CARMEN BASILIO: "You'd be amazed how many business propositions you get for going into business, and it's funny that all these businesses need money . . . your money. You get propositions from a peanut stand to a bowling alley. It is only in recent fights that I started to make real good pay days. I fought too hard for that money to sink it into businesses I know nothing about. My wife, Kay, is smarter than I am. She has a tremendous instinct for what's good for me and what isn't. I'm grateful too, to my co-managers, Joe Nitro and Johnny DeJohn . . . they are my watchdogs."

The new champion was not concerned about his ninety-day rematch clause with Sugar Ray Robinson. He was still upset over being leveraged by him on his percentages in the first fight. Robinson took home $483,666 to Basilio's $215,629. The new champion bristled at the difference in the two purses. He had his best payday of his career with Robinson, but that didn't diminish the disdain he had for him. He held the cards this time around, and he was going to hold Sugar Ray's feet to the fire. Sugar Ray, with his mounting tax problems, needed money. There was no other fight available for either of them that could generate the gate that this odd couple could generate.

CARMEN BASILIO: "He took the big money the first time, but he's getting nothing this time. He can make all the demands that he wants but he won't get all he wants this time. They were talking about a fight in Chicago, in February, but to tell you the truth, I don't care if we have it or not."

George Gainford had complained throughout the fight to referee Al Beryl that the ointment Angelo Dundee was using on Basilio's bleeding left brow was getting into Robinson's eyes, causing him discomfort and his eyes to water. "I'd like to see Ray fight Basilio for the title again. If we can get assurances from the boxing commission that the New York State law against the use of collodion-iodoform ointment will be carried out."

Basilio, when told of Gainford's accusations, said Sugar Ray's trainer was "full of shit." He questioned the logic of Gainford's assertion: "If it got in his eyes, how come it didn't get in mine? Angelo [Dundee] has been using the same ointment on me for years, and this is the first time somebody has complained about it. I'd say its sour grapes on his part."

Sugar Ray Robinson, following his loss to Basilio, had suggested that he might not fight again. In his mind he was going to fight Basilio, he was going to take a few days to recover, and then go about the business of arranging the second fight. Nobody had ever beat him twice, and besides the money, there was the challenge of doing something no one else in boxing had ever done: win the title five times.

The second installment for Basilio-Robinson was set for Chicago Stadium on March 25, 1958. Each fighter would receive 30 percent of the gross receipts, including the closed-circuit television revenues. Sugar Ray, given his financial problems, had contracted the fight under his new company, Robinson Theater and Sports Promotion Corporation. The money earned from this fight would be paid out over a four-year period. Both fighters indicated they expected another tough battle while preparing for a long fight. Basilio trained in Miami at Angelo Dundee's Fifth Street Gym before heading to Chicago a few days prior to the fight. Basilio thought he had given Robinson too much ring to work with in their first fight, vowing to cut the size of the ring down by a third. He said he had miscalculated Sugar Ray's stamina, believing that the more ground he covered, the quicker he would tire.

CARMEN BASILIO: "At the time of my Yankee Stadium fight with Ray, I figured that I knew all about him as a fighter. It seems I didn't. When the final bell rang he was still fighting at the end. He tired but not enough or fast enough. Robinson knows I can beat him. That's very important. Ray knows it and so do I . . . that is also important. I have it in stamina and in determination. I have not been spoiled by too many heavy paydays. Robinson is considerably older . . . he is at an age when fighters think of ease and retirement."

Sugar Ray Robinson looked sharp in his final hard workout preceding the fight, knocking down one of his sparring partners with a blistering left-right combination. Physically, he was in good condition and confident he would win back the crown. Chicago had been good to Robinson, having won eleven out of twelve matches there with the only blemish his fight with Tiger Jones in 1955. He was undefeated in rematches and planned on extending that streak against Basilio. Sugar Ray's close friend Frank Sinatra was flying to Chicago to lend his moral support. When a writer mentioned to Basilio that Robinson's pal Sinatra was attending the fight, Basilio shot back, "How's that gonna help Robinson?"

•   •   •

CHICAGO, MARCH 25, 1958. Carmen Basilio weighed in at 153 pounds, 6½ pounds lighter than his opponent. Sugar Ray, at 162 pounds the day before the fight, had to go without food for twenty hours to make the 160-pound limit. Basilio was the slight favorite at 6-5 as the two boxers entered the ring. The fight, taking place in Illinois, would be scored on a five-point Must System. A fighter would earn five points for each round he won. His opponent could earn up to four points depending on how each judge and referee scored his performance. When a round was considered even, each fighter would receive five points.

Howard Cosell spoke with the champion following the weigh-in: "Carmen, in all the excitement of the weigh-in . . . just one question. I polled ten sportswriters from around the nation here and nine of them pick Sugar Ray by knockout tonight. What's your answer?" Carmen shot back, "Nine of them are wrong!"

When the bell rang to begin the rematch for the middleweight title, the champion exploded out of his corner, landing body shot after body shot. Basilio, through the first nine minutes of action, won two of the first three rounds. Late in the third round, Robinson scored with a solid left hook, which opened a small cut at the side of Basilio's nose. In the fifth round, Robinson shook Basilio with a hard left-right combination that caused some puffiness to

Carmen's left eye. By the seventh round the left eye was closing and beginning to balloon out. Robinson continued to pepper Carmen's face with left jabs through the eighth, but the game Basilio kept wading in, absorbing a tremendous amount of punishment. In the ninth round the two fighters again traded punches before Basilio ducked under a right hand, rocking Robinson with a solid left hook to the head, followed by a right-left combination to the body . . . winning the round. The tenth and eleventh rounds saw Basilio again score with solid body shots that forced Robinson to cover up, clearly feeling the effects of the punches.

Between rounds George Gainford challenged Sugar Ray to step it up; Robinson was letting Basilio back into the fight. "He's got your title . . . attack him. He's hurt . . . he's tired . . . he's ready to go . . . don't let him outwork you!"

Robinson stormed back in the twelfth, tracking Basilio around the ring, jabbing his left eye over and over while working his body with solid left and rights. Robinson regained control of the fight, bombing Basilio with combinations to the head and body. In the fifteenth, after being accidentally butted, Robinson hit Basilio with a right to the jaw that made his body quiver. Robinson remained on the attack, buckling Basilio's knees with a perfect three-punch combination. Somehow, Basilio remained standing, staying on his feet and battling as best he could as the bell clanged to end the fight.

Judge John Bray voted it 71-64, Robinson. Referee Frank Sikora scored it 69-66, Basilio. Judge Frank McAdams had it 72-64, Robinson. Sugar Ray Robinson had, incredibly, won the middleweight championship back for a record fifth time. In another tough, hard-fought, close fight, he had come out victorious. In a poll at ringside of thirty writers following the fight, twenty-eight thought Robinson had won. On rounds, referee Sikora had it 9-5-1, Basilio. Judge Bray had it 11-4, Robinson. Judge McAdams had it 11-3-1, Robinson.

FRANK SIKORA (Referee): "I gave it to Basilio because he made the fight. He carried it to Robinson and fought three minutes of every round. Robinson was a spot fighter, coasting much of the time. I scored it in Basilio's favor because he was scoring with body punches. Robinson's only real big round was the last. Basilio had Robinson in a bad way three or four times with his persistent attack. I'm on top of the action all the time, closer to the fight than anybody. I voted the way I saw it and the judges voted the way they saw it. I thought Basilio won."

The fight had exacted a huge toll on both fighters. Basilio, his left eye the size of a discolored billiard ball, would land in the hospital. Robinson, in winning the fight, had to be helped to his dressing room by his handlers. He barred newsmen from meeting with him for more than an hour. Later, it was announced that Sugar Ray wouldn't be able to speak with the writers at the arena. The disgruntled press corps was told that Sugar Ray would meet with them at his hotel room. The new middleweight champion, lying in his hotel bed, described his thoughts about his opponent, their fight, and his future: "He was very tough. This was one of the toughest fights I have ever had. I am so tired . . . I feel like ten guys jumped on me. I pretty near am aching in every bone. I don't know at this time if I will fight again."

In his locker room, his head down, spitting blood into a pail, an ice pack on his injured eye, a sobbing Carmen Basilio asked James Norris to get him a repeat bout. The game fighter had displayed amazing courage, battling the last eight rounds half-blind, refusing to give in to the pain and the impossible odds of winning. He was there to fight, to do his best . . . there was a reason people loved him. He always gave his best no matter what. Quitting was never part of his makeup. He'd fight to the bitter end regardless of which side of the fence he was on.

CARMEN BASILIO: "He didn't hurt me at any time. Were it not for this eye damage, I would have repeated. I don't think I lost. I beat him once and I could do it again."

ANGELO DUNDEE (Basilio Cornerman): "I wanted to cut his eye but I couldn't because the bleeding was internal, right next to the eyeball. Hey, I'm no surgeon. I had the razor blade ready in my pocket but couldn't use it. All I could do was apply ice between rounds. When *Sports Illustrated* said that he was the only guy in a million that could have withstood what he went through . . . they were wrong. He's the only guy period that could have handled that and kept going . . . he's one of a kind."

DR. RICHARD PERRITT (Chicago Eye Specialist): "The eye itself is not involved . . . there has been a massive hemorrhage around the eye and we want Mr. Basilio to be hospitalized several days for observation and treatment."

Sugar Ray Robinson returned to New York City the following morning, telling the press that he was weighing his options regarding fighting again. He had no plans in the immediate future about whom he might fight or when it would happen. Sugar Ray said he would have to give "some thought" to a third fight with Basilio. He mentioned a possible screen test, saying that he had read a movie script about a Mexican bullfighter whom he had some interest in playing. Robinson also reported that there was a chance that the IRS would hold up his purse. Each fighter was to receive $256,469 as his share of the gate, radio rights, and movie and theater television fees.

James Norris and the IBC were saddled with a complaint from Gene Fullmer's manager, Marv Jensen, who was threatening a $1 million lawsuit if Fullmer was not Robinson's next opponent. Jensen's contention was that Fullmer had a signed agreement to fight the winner of the Basilio-Robinson bout the previous September in Yankee Stadium. The IBC said that a letter of agreement signed by James Norris and Truman Gibson was not a legal contract.

ARTHUR DALEY (Writer): "For five rounds Basilio mistreated Ray, not that Robinson didn't get in some pretty good licks himself. But the superlatively equipped Harlemite is a deadly hitter as well as a boxer of consummate skill. Just before the end of the fifth he landed the one punch that won the fight. It wasn't that apparent when it landed, but the effects became increasingly obvious. Basilio hooked into the body savagely and had Robinson in distress. That's when Sugar Ray is most dangerous. He came out of a clinch with bomb bays open. A left hook flashed joltingly on Carmen's jaw and a right exploded on Carmen's head. It landed on Carmen's left eye and that won the war."

36. *(Left to right):* Carmen Basilio, Greg Sorrentino, and Johnny DeJohn. *Courtesy of Greg Sorrentino.*

15.

Between Rounds

donnie HAMILTON: "I was fifteen years old when Irv Robbins got me a boxing license. At that time you had to be seventeen to box in New York. Matter of fact, I used that same license to join the National Guard. They had my picture on it, very professional. Anyway, he gets me this license, and I'm able to box. I'm standing in line for the weigh-in, I'm nervous, I'm fifteen, I probably looked twelve. I'm looking at all the fighters weighing in, seeing which one is my size. I'm looking at this guy right ahead of me, he looks about my size, a little taller than me. More mature, hair on his chest. I said to Irv, 'Am I boxing that guy?' Irv says, 'Yeah . . . Why?' I said, 'Can he fight?' He says, 'If he could fight, he wouldn't be fighting you!'"

JOSIE BASILIO (Wife): "I met Carmen in August 1980, at the Italian Festival in Rochester, New York, when he was working for the Genesee Brewery in public relations. Being Italian, of course I knew he was champion of the world at one time. What I instantly liked about him was that he was very friendly, a fun person to be around. He likes people. He is a very gentle person. He's like a little lamb."

TONY LICCIONE (Rochester Boxing Hall of Fame): "Carmen Basilio is the real deal. He is the most courageous fighter in the history of boxing and one of the finest people I have ever met in my life."

JOSIE BASILIO (Wife): "Carmen is one of the most loyal people you will ever meet. When he worked for the Genesee Brewery,

191

37. Carmen and Josie Basilio. *Courtesy of Carmen Basilio.*

if people came to the house and brought some other type of beer, he'd tell them to take their empty bottles with them when they left. 'Don't leave any of that stuff here. I work for the Genesee Brewing Company. You think if one of my big bosses stops by the house I would have some other kind of beer to offer them? No way.'"

BERNARD WINEBURG (Friend): "Carmen was very good friends with Joe DiMaggio. I remember I went to Chicago with him, and we had dinner with Joe. I had Joe DiMaggio on my left and Carmen Basilio on my right. It doesn't get much better than that."

LESLIE WINEBURG (Friend): "We were visiting Carmen and Josie in Rochester, and we went out to dinner at this lovely Italian restaurant. When we sat down there was a group of about twelve people at the next table. When they realized it was Carmen, they all came over asking for his autograph and asking if he would pose for

38. Carmen and Josie Basilio with Leslie and Bernard Wineburg.
Courtesy of Bernard Wineburg.

a picture. Josie says to them, 'If you will allow us to have our dinner and talk with our friends, we will be happy to meet you afterwards in the lounge. Carmen will be happy to sign autographs and have his picture taken with you—whatever you want.' Well, they are at the next table watching us. Eventually, I have to get up and go to the bathroom. So, I get up and go, and all the women at the table follow me to the bathroom. 'Are you Carmen's daughter? Who are you to them? Tell us about how Carmen is really like.' After dinner Carmen was very gracious with them. He signed autographs and had pictures taken with them. He was wonderful."

JAMES J. BRADDOCK (Boxer): "Carmen Basilio has a punch. He's a real banger, and he wins respect with his banging. He whittles them guys down to size where they don't think about hitting him. They think about protecting themselves. That's why Robinson ran so much when they fought."

ADA ROTHSCHILD (Wife): "When Norm was going to first use Carmen, everyone said, 'You're going to lose your shirt.' He wasn't the colorful fighter that Mike DeJohn or Joey DeJohn were at that time. But his style changed under Johnny DeJohn. He had a heart like no other fighter. He wouldn't let them lick him. I saw him after fights where his eyes were blown up like you couldn't believe. Johnny and Carmen were a good pairing."

ANGELO DUNDEE (Basilio Cornerman): "Basilio almost got me arrested in Chicago. We got up early so he can do his road-work. I take him out to the lakefront. I'm standing there waiting for him to come back, and a patrol car pulls up. This big cop gets out and asks me what I'm doing out here at this time of the day. He says there has been some burglaries around this area. I tell him why I'm here . . . I'm waiting for my fighter to come back from his roadwork. He waits with me, but Carmen doesn't return. Now, I'm getting nervous because the cop's getting impatient, and I'm wondering if something bad happened to Carmen. Finally, the cop tells me to get the hell out of here and don't come back. I get in the car, and Carmen is in the back of the car laughing his ass off. Somehow he sneaked in the car without me or the officer seeing him. He loved to break balls."

JIMMY CANNON (Writer): "Once I was awakened by a phone call from Rocky Graziano. 'Come on over to Stillman's. I got a scoop for you.' I dressed rapidly and was grasping for breath after running up the stairs. A guy in a zoot suit under a big hat was wait-ing for me and steered me back into the dressing room, where Gra-ziano sat on a rubbing table. 'Go,' he said to another guy who wore blue working pants and was naked from the waist up. The guy held a harmonica against his nostrils and blew the breath out of his nose. Slowly, the harmonica wheezed 'Swanee River.' 'The only man in the world who could play "Swanee River," with his nose,' Graziano said when the concert was over. 'He could make a million dollars.' The guy stood there, proud and smiling, and the middleweight champion of the world slapped him on the back and requested an encore. Years afterward there was an underworld outfit called the Gallos, who were getting big play in the papers. They had chal-lenged the Mafia, and I had wondered who they were. 'You know them,' Graziano said. 'Remember the guy in the zoot suit brought you back to hear the jerk play the harmonica with his nose? That was one of the Gallos.'"

DONNIE HAMILTON (Boxing Historian): "I remembering meeting Art Aragon a year after he had fought Carmen [in 1958]. I asked him if he would fight Basilio again. He said, 'Sure, I'd fight Basilio again—if they let me go in the ring with a gun, then I'll fight him again.'"

ART ARAGON: "I made eighty grand for the Basilio fight. Unfortunately, it cost me ninety grand to get out of the hospital."

GREG SORRENTINO (Boxer): "Billy Backus, Carmen's nephew, was fighting Hedgemon Lewis at the War Memorial [in Syracuse]. Billy was a southpaw, and southpaws fight best moving to their right. Billy was moving into his left and getting hit by lead right hands. Carmen runs up to the corner and yelled at Tony Graziano [Backus's manager], 'Tell that kid to move to his right.' Graziano said, 'Mind your own business.' Carmen dropped him right there with a right hand—his glasses hanging off his nose all crooked and stuff. Later they reconciled that relationship."

CUS D'AMATO: "You have no idea what kind of people you're dealing with in this business. I don't believe a word they say. I want it in writing. Maybe that's why they call me Cautious Cus. One New York sportswriter called me a psychopath. He should have to put up with my troubles."

ADA ROTHSCHILD (Wife): "One thing Gene Fullmer and Carmen Basilio had in common was their mothers. They both were tough."

JIMMY CANNON (Writer): "There was an afternoon when Tom Kelly, a fight manager, told me he wanted to be described by the name on his birth certificate. He was born Tony Leto. He was standing near a phone when another manager answered it. 'What Tom Kelly you want?' the guy asked. 'The Italian one . . . the Irish one . . . the Jewish one?'"

CARMEN BASILIO: "The greatest thrill I ever got in my life was in the ring at the War Memorial in Syracuse, New York, on the night June 10, 1955, when they raised my hand as the new welterweight champion of the world. You can't explain those things. The thrill will never leave me."

GREG SORRENTINO (Boxer): "Carmen Basilio should be in the dictionary under *fighter* . . . there should just be a picture of Carmen. That's the bottom line. I have never met anybody so driven who trained himself to be a champion. His kind of physical conditioning coupled with hunger and focus is a formidable thing."

CARMEN SCIALABBA (Boxer): "When I was in the marines my boxing coach was Jerry Plunkett, who was good friends with Carmen Basilio. I told Jerry that I wanted to give boxing a try when I got out of the marines, and he hooked me up with Carmen Basilio. I moved to Syracuse and began to work out with Carmen. . . . His workouts were unbelievable . . . nobody could keep up with him. He was the hardest worker I have ever seen. In 1959, I had a fight scheduled in Butler, Pennsylvania, outdoors at this baseball field. Leading up to the fight, I was having trouble breathing, and I had a pain in my chest. Also I was sweating a lot. I didn't say anything to Carmen, but he could tell I wasn't right. It rained, and the fight was canceled. I had planned to stay in Pennsylvania and spend some time with my family, but Carmen insisted that I come back with him to Syracuse. The next morning, he makes an appointment for me to see his doctor. I tell him I'm not going . . . there is nothing wrong with me. He says, 'You're going. Now do you want to do it the easy way, or do you want to do it the hard way?' So, we go to the hospital, and they do a spinal tap. Later, Carmen comes into my room, and I can see his eyes are bloodshot, and he says, 'You have to stay in the hospital, my friend. The doctor believes you have polio.' A few hours later, I was paralyzed from the waist down. If Carmen hadn't insisted I go to Syracuse with him and then to the hospital, I would have died. I had planned to stay at this apartment in Butler and would have been there by myself. Carmen Basilio is the most caring person I have ever met in my life. He is a far greater champion outside the ring than he was inside the ring. He cares deeply about people. When I was fighting professionally and he was my manager, he never took a dime from me. When we were on the road, he would pay all the expenses . . . that's the kind of guy Carmen is. He is the most unassuming person you will ever meet, for all that he has accomplished in his life."

Author's note: Carmen Scialabba went on to get his bachelor of science degree from the University of Pittsburgh and his master's degree from Indiana University in Pennsylvania. He worked for seven years on Capitol Hill for Congressman John Murtha and now is a consultant in Washington, D.C. He resides in Silver Spring, Maryland. Carmen Basilio is godfather to his daughter . . . named Carmen.

Epilogue

Many people ask why I keep fighting. Do I need the money? Yes, I need the money but it isn't my main goal. I believe I will be victorious in another championship fight and retire as the middleweight champion of the world.
—SUGAR RAY ROBINSON, *circa 1964*

Carmen Basilio and Sugar Ray Robinson never got back in the ring together. All the talk of a third bout was just that— talk. The intensity and courage each man displayed, through thirty rounds of fighting, had fight fans worldwide hoping for a third go-round between these two bitter rivals. Robinson, after being hit thirty-four straight times in the eleventh round of the first fight, mystified his critics by almost knocking Basilio out and dominating the last four rounds. In the second encounter, Basilio, a cyclops figure, fought half-blind for the majority of the fight, telling Angelo Dundee in the fourteenth round, "If you stop the fight, you had better be out of town when I leave the ring." The resolve of both boxers was head-shaking: two guys different in so many ways yet so alike in their distaste for losing.

Philosophically, each man approached life from a different perspective. Ultimately, they both wanted the same things from boxing—wealth, respect, a comfortable retirement—and both were determined to arrive at that destination . . . they just took different roads to get there. For Sugar Ray, it was important to exact his will in every aspect of his life, whether in the ring, in his marriage, or in negotiations for a fight. It was a simple belief devoid of greed or selfishness. One person had to win! He spent little time worrying about the ramifications of his actions, sensitive to the criticism but strong-willed enough to follow his own convictions. Over a lifetime, his beliefs had taken him to the top of the sport. Sugar Ray never understood why some writers bashed him for perceived cockiness, which he attributed to confidence in himself. Being evasive or unavailable to the press never endeared him to boxing writers who had columns to write and deadlines to meet. No promoter in the world would *not* want to promote one of his fights, but he could drive them insane with his unending requests. A renowned "run-out artist" on fights, he would defend his actions by saying he had a responsibility to be physically and mentally prepared in order to give his best to win. He justified these actions by saying that they were "in the best interests of the sport, and himself." He was adored in the ring for his immense talent, but few people close to boxing liked him. He could turn on the charm or be mean and calculating, unaware of another's presence. A devout Christian and a supporter of many causes, especially when it concerned the advancement of his own race, he was a man of many moods and descriptions. He was the best boxer, "pound for pound," we have ever seen. In achieving his goals, he misjudged his actions and intention that forced him to stay much longer in a sport he said he detested. In the latter years of his life he suffered from diabetes, hypertension, arteriosclerosis, and Alzheimer's disease. A number of years before his death, he said one of the biggest mistakes he made in his career was not fighting Carmen Basilio a third time.

JIMMY CANNON (Writer): "It is normal for people to resent imperfection in a man who does something better than anyone else alive . . . that is why Robinson rarely measures up to the image created by his public performances."

Carmen Basilio realized his lifelong dream of becoming a champion: fighting great fighters in great fights. Meeting Sugar Ray in the ring was more than just fighting for a big payday and the middleweight title; it was about gaining back the respect that

Robinson had taken when he "dissed" Carmen years before. A proud man, Basilio approached fights with a work ethic few in the history of the game could match. He was a man with simple values who believed in treating others the way he wanted to be treated; like his sharecropper father before him, he believed in "one onion for you and one onion for me." Basilio resented Robinson for wanting more.

In negotiations, prior to Basilio and Robinson ever appearing in a ring together, it was prearranged for Carmen to receive only 20 percent for a first bout, an even split on a second, with Robinson receiving 42.5 percent for a third matchup. Basilio, frustrated with Robinson wanting to renegotiate a bigger split for the third fight, wasn't about to take a financial "dive" this time around. Some people thought it was a ploy by Robinson to avoid a third time in the ring with Basilio.

The last fight in Chicago on March 25, 1958, signaled the beginning of the end for both fighters—neither would win another championship. Did the epic battle between them take a toll on both fighters? No one can say for certain.

Sugar Ray, deep in debt, with his businesses quickly failing, was forced to do what he did best: box. He would continue in the ring for another seven and a half years, fighting fifty-two more times but winning only thirty-four of those matches. On November 10, 1965, in Pittsburgh, Robinson fought for the last time, losing to Joey Archer. There would be no more comebacks. He was forty-four years old.

Carmen Basilio fought seven more times, winning four and losing three. In his last fight, on April 22, 1961, in Boston, Basilio was defeated by Paul Pender while trying to regain the middleweight title. He was thirty-four years old. He went on to work at Le Moyne College in Syracuse as a physical education instructor while also making public appearances for the Genesee Brewing Company. He remarried in 1986 and lives in Rochester with his second wife, Josie. Both are active with the International Boxing Hall of Fame, in Carmen's hometown of Canastota, New York.

The Essence of Carmen Basilio

Roll Call

Career Statistics, 56-16-7

Bibliography

The Essence of Carmen Basilio

GARY YOUMANS: What was your toughest fight?

CARMEN BASILIO: My wife. She beat me six times.

GY: Tell me about your mother.

CB: She was four feet ten. She had ten babies. That was before television.

GY: What was your father like?

CB: He was a hardworking man. He could be very strict. He could be tough—he kicked my ass a few times. He was very religious . . . a good guy, a hardworking man . . . With ten kids he had to be that way. He was poor his whole life. Worked like a slave. When I could afford it I paid off his mortgage and took him places. He was in his glory.

GY: What is your favorite meal?

CB: Food. A good steak dinner is beautiful. A nice spaghetti dinner cooked by my wife, Josie, is beautiful.

GY: What is your favorite movie?

CB: Favorite movie? I don't have a favorite movie . . . I go to sleep.

GY: Why do you think people enjoyed watching you fight so much?

CB: When people buy a fight ticket, they're paying to see blood and knockdowns. Every time I go into the ring I expect to be busted up. It is as much a part of the business as the boxing gloves. There is no room in the ring for two fighters, a referee, and pity. It's him or me.

GY: Has anyone ever approached you about throwing a fight?

CB: If ever anybody approached me about a bribe to throw a fight I would have them arrested. First I would punch them in the nose, and then I would have them arrested.

GY: Do you ever worry about getting hurt in the ring?

CB: I was never afraid of getting hurt in the ring. That's what fighting is all about. If you're going to give it out, then you have got to take it too.

GY: When you look back on your life, what would you change?

CB: Nothing. I would change nothing. I have had a good life.

Roll Call

Gabe Genovese was convicted of being an unlicensed manager in 1958. It was reported that he had collected close to seventy thousand dollars from John DeJohn and Joe Nitro over a three-year period, beginning in 1955. He was the middleman for Frankie Carbo on these transactions. Before Genovese was sentenced, the assistant district attorney, John G. Bonomi, referred to him as "an evil and degrading influence on professional boxing for over two decades." Genovese was sentenced to two years in Rikers Penitentiary. He served just over one year before being released. He died soon after.

Frankie Carbo, the "underworld commissioner of boxing," was sentenced in New York to two years in Rikers Penitentiary in November 1959. The charges included being an unlicensed manager and an unlicensed matchmaker and conspiracy.

In December 1961, in a Los Angeles federal court, Frankie Carbo, Blinky Palermo, and Truman Gibson were found guilty of extortion and conspiracy charges. Carbo was sentenced to twenty-five years in prison and fined ten thousand dollars. Given early parole, he died in 1976. He was seventy-two years old.

SCOTTI (assistant district attorney): I believe it is fair to say that the name of Frankie Carbo today symbolizes the degeneration of professional boxing into a racket. This man is beyond redemption. The evil influence of this man has for many years permeated virtually the entire sport of boxing. He is completely impervious to public opinion.

Blinky Palermo was sentenced to fifteen years and a ten thousand–dollar fine. He died in 1996. He was ninety-one years old.

Truman Gibson was sentenced to five years in prison and a five thousand–dollar fine. His sentence was suspended. He died in 2006. He was ninety-three years old.

Arthur M. Wirtz died in 1982 of cancer. He was eighty-one years old.

James D. Norris died of heart failure in 1966. He was fifty-nine years old, with a reported net worth of $250 million.

Norm Rothschild died in Syracuse in January 1988. He was sixty-eight years old.

George Gainford died in New York in 1981.

John DeJohn died in Syracuse in 2001. He was eighty-seven years old.

Joe Nitro died in 1970. He was sixty-four years old.

Sugar Ray Robinson died in 1989. He was sixty-seven years old.

Kid Gavilan died in Miami of a heart attack in February 2003.

Joe Louis died in April 1981. He was seventy-three years old.

Mary Basilio died in 1985 at the age of ninety-one.

Joseph Basilio died in August 1974. He was eighty-eight years old.

Tony DeMarco still lives in New England.

Carmen Basilio Career Statistics, 56-16-7

1948

November 24	Jimmy Evans	Binghamton	KO3
November 29	Bruce Walters	Syracuse	KO1
December 8	Eddie Thomas	Binghamton	KO2
December 16	Rollie Johns	Syracuse	W6

1949

January 5	Johnny Cunningham	Binghamton	D6
January 19	Jay Perlin	Binghamton	D6
January 25	Ernie Hall	Syracuse	KO2
February 19	Luke Jordan	Rochester	W6
April 20	Elliott Throop	Syracuse	KO1
May 2	Connie Thies	Rochester	L6
May 8	Jerry Drain	Syracuse	KO3
May 18	Johnny Clemons	Syracuse	KO3
June 7	Johnny Cunningham	Syracuse	KO2
July 12	Jesse Bradshaw	Syracuse	KO2
July 21	Sammy Daniels	Utica	W8
August 2	Johnny Cunningham	Utica	L8
August 17	Johnny Cunningham	Syracuse	W8
September 7	Tony DiPelino	Rochester	W8
September 30	Jackie Parker	Syracuse	KO3

1950

| January 10 | Sonny Hampton | Buffalo | W8 |

January 24	Cassill Tate	Buffalo	W8
February 7	Adrien Mourguiart	Buffalo	KO7
March 6	Lew Jenkins	Syracuse	W10
March 27	Mike Koballa	Brooklyn	L8
April 12	Gaby Ferland	New Orleans	D10
May 5	Gaby Ferland	New Orleans	KO1
June 21	Guillermo Giminez	New Orleans	KO8
July 31	Guillermo Giminez	New Orleans	KO9
August 28	Eddie Giosa	New Orleans	L10
December 15	Vic Cardell	New York	L10

1951

March 9	Floro Hita	Syracuse	W8
April 12	Eddie Giosa	Syracuse	W10
May 29	Lester Felton	Syracuse	L10
June 18	Johnny Cesario	Utica	L10
September 17	Shamus McCray	Syracuse	W8
September 26	Ross Virgo	New Orleans	L10

1952

February 4	Emmett Norris	Wilkes-Barre	W10
February 28	Jimmy Cousins	Akron	W8
March 31	Jackie O'Brien	Wilkes-Barre	W10
May 29	Chuck Davey	Syracuse	D10
July 16	Chuck Davey	Chicago	L10
August 20	Billy Graham	Chicago	L10
September 22	Baby Williams	Miami	W10
October 20	Sammy Guiliani	Syracuse	KO3
November 18	Chuck Foster	Buffalo	KO5

1953

January 12	Ike Williams	Syracuse	W10
February 28	Vic Cardell	Toledo	W10

April 11	Carmine Fiore	Syracuse	KO9
June 6	Billy Graham	Syracuse	W12
June 25	Billy Graham	Syracuse	D12
September 18	Kid Gavilan	Syracuse	L15[1]
November 28	Johnny Cunnignham	Toledo	KO4
December 19	Pierre Langlois	Syracuse	D10

1954

January 16	Italo Scortichini	Miami	D10
April 17	Pierre Langlois	Syracuse	W10
May 15	Italo Scortichini	Syracuse	W10
June 26	Al Andrews	Syracuse	W10
August 17	Ronnie Harper	Fort Wayne	KO2
September 10	Carmine Fiore	New York	W10
October 15	Allie Gronik	Syracuse	W10
December 16	Ronnie Harper	Akron	KO4

1955

January 21	Peter Muller	Syracuse	W10
June 10	Tony DeMarco	Syracuse	KO12[2]
August 10	Italo Scortichini	New York	W10
September 7	Gil Turner	Syracuse	W10
November 30	Tony DeMarco	Boston	KO12[3]

1956

March 14	Johnny Saxton	Chicago	L15[4]
September 12	Johnny Saxton	Syracuse	KO9[5]

1. For World Welterweight Championship.
2. Won World Welterweight Championship.
3. Retained World Welterweight Championship.
4. Lost World Welterweight Championship.
5. Regained World Welterweight Championship.

1957

February 22	Johnny Saxton	Cleveland	KO2[6]
May 13	Leo Owens	Longview, OR	Exh 3
May 14	Leo Owens	Spokane	Exh 3
May 16	Harold Jones	Portland	KO4
June 27	Leo Owens	Jeanette, PA	Exh 3
September 23	Ray Robinson	New York	W15[7]

1958

March 25	Ray Robinson	Chicago	L15[8]
September 5	Art Aragon	Los Angeles	KO8

1959

April 1	Arley Selfer	Augusta	KO3
August 28	Gene Fullmer	San Francisco	KO'd 14[9]

1960

June 29	Gene Fullmer	Salt Lake City	KO'd 12[10]

1961

January 7	Gaspar Ortega	New York	W10
March 11	Don Jordan	Syracuse	W10
April 22	Paul Pender	Boston	L10[11]

6. Retained World Welterweight Championship.

7. Won World Middleweight Championship; gave up World Welterweight Championship.

8. Lost World Middleweight Championship.

9. For NBA Middleweight Championship.

10. For NBA Middleweight Championship.

11. For World Middleweight Championship.

Bibliography

Books

Anderson, Dave, ed. *The Red Smith Reader*. New York: Random House, 1982.

Boyd, Herb, and Ray Robinson II. *A Biography of Sugar Ray Robinson: Pound for Pound*. Amistad, 2005.

Brenner, Teddy, and Barney Nagler. *Only the Ring Was Square*. Englewood Cliffs, N.J.: Prentice-Hall, 1981.

Cannon, Jack, and Tom Cannon. *Nobody Asked Me, But: The World of Jimmy Cannon*. New York: Holt, Rinehart, and Winston, 1978.

Fitzgerald, Mike. 2004. *The Ageless Warrior: The Life of Boxing Legend Archie Moore*. Sports Publishing.

Fried, Ronald K. 1991. *Corner Men*. New York: Four Walls Eight Windows.

Halberstam, David. 1993. *The Fifties*. New York: Villard Books.

La Motta, Jake. *Raging Bull*.

Myler, Patrick. 1997. *A Century of Boxing Greats*. Park West, N.Y.: Robson Books.

Nagler, Barney. 1964. *James Norris and the Decline of Boxing*. Indianapolis: Bobbs-Merrill.

Roberts, James B., and Alexander G. Skutt. 1997. *The Boxing Register: The International Boxing Hall of Fame Official Record Book*. Ithaca: McBooks Press.

Articles

"Basilio Wants Fullmer." *Ring Magazine,* May 1957.

"Basilio Was a Name for Courage." *Boxing International,* Sept. 1965.

"Blood Bath in Boston." *Boxing Illustrated*, Jan. 1960.

"Can Basilio Keep from Getting Hurt?" *Sport Magazine*, Feb. 1958.

"Club Fighter." *Boxing Yearbook*, 1953.

"God Makes a Champion." *Boxing and Wrestling Magazine*, Aug. 1957.

"How You Build a Champion." *Boxing Yearbook*, 1953.

"I Got the Business," by Kid Gavilan. *Boxing and Wrestling*, Mar. 1955.

"Inside Carmen Basilio." *Boxing Yearbook*, 1955.

"Intimate Slants on Basilio." *Ring Magazine*, Mar. 1958.

"I Want the Middleweight Title." *Ringside Magazine*, Dec. 1955.

"Last Seconds of a Champion." *Sports Illustrated*, Jan. 14, 1957.

"The Man from Utah." *Ring Magazine*, Mar. 1957.

"A Mighty Peculiar Fight." *Sports Illustrated*, Mar. 26, 1956.

"The Potent Left Hook." *Ring Magazine*, Oct. 1957.

"Ray-Ray for Ray." *Ring Magazine*, Mar. 1955.

"Robinson-Olsen Upset of the Year." *Ring Magazine*, 1956.

"Saxton's Reward." *Sports Illustrated*, Mar. 26, 1956.

"Supreme Court Decision Changes Boxing Scene." *Ring Magazine*, Mar. 1959.

"Terror: 342 Seconds with Basilio." *Sports Illustrated*, Jan. 1957.

"Will Robinson Win Middle Title for Fifth Time?" *Ring Magazine*, 1958.

"Worshipped—Not Liked." *Ring Magazine*, Apr. 1959.